Successful Inclusion Strategies

for Early Childhood Teachers

Successful Inclusion Strategies

Strategies for Early Childhood Teachers

Cynthia G. Simpson, Ph.D.
and Laverne Warner, Ph.D.

Prufrock Press Inc.
Waco, Texas

Library of Congress Cataloging-in-Publication Data

Simpson, Cynthia G.
  Successful inclusion strategies for early childhood teachers / Cynthia G. Simpson and Laverne Warner.
    p. cm.
  Includes bibliographical references.
  ISBN 978-1-59363-383-7 (pbk.)
  1. Inclusive education--United States. 2. Children with disabilities--Education (Early childhood)--United States.
  3. Early childhood education. I. Warner, Laverne, 1941- II. Title.
  LC1201.S545 2010
  371.9'046--dc22
                      2009032576

Copyright © 2010, Prufrock Press Inc.
Edited by Lacy Compton
Cover and Layout Design by Marjorie Parker

ISBN-13: 978-1-59363-383-7
ISBN-10: 1-59363-383-1

Printed in the United States of America.

At the time of this book's publication, all facts and figures cited are the most current available. All telephone numbers, addresses, and Web site URLs are accurate and active. All publications, organizations, Web sites, and other resources exist as described in the book, and all have been verified. The authors and Prufrock Press Inc. make no warranty or guarantee concerning the information and materials given out by organizations or content found at Web sites, and we are not responsible for any changes that occur after this book's publication. If you find an error, please contact Prufrock Press Inc.

Prufrock Press Inc.
P.O. Box 8813
Waco, TX 76714-8813
Phone: (800) 998-2208
Fax: (800) 240-0333
http://www.prufrock.com

DEDICATED TO

Robert Alan Simpson
Christopher Matthew Simpson
Jacqueline Nicole Simpson

Delton Warner Phelps
Zoey Lauren Hill
Molly Kate Hill

Contents

CHAPTER **10**

CHAPTER **11**

CHAPTER **12**

Acknowledgements

The authors wish to thank the following individuals for reading our manuscript and providing feedback:

- Sharon Lynch and Vicky Spencer, Colleagues from Sam Houston State University and George Mason University
- Doris Warner Phelps, Retired elementary school principal, Conroe Independent School District, Conroe, TX
- Sally Jane Pittman, Adjunct Professor, Angelina College

Introduction

Have you had one or more of the following classroom experiences?

- You try to get the children's attention, but one child stands out from the rest and does not seem to know that he is part of the group.
- You notice that one of the children in your class seems pre-occupied with her hands every time you read a book to the class while the other children respond to the reading with pleasure.
- A child in your class has frequent emotional outbursts at unusual times during the day that are not consistent with typical, age-appropriate outbursts.
- A parent of a child in your classroom has mentioned a physical impairment her child has and is seeking additional information on how to support your teaching in the home setting.

Most teachers have received some information regarding children with special needs in workshop sessions or conferences, in professional journals, newspapers, or even on television news programs. Having an awareness of disabilities is the first step in helping to meet the needs of all of the children in your class and their families. Your purchase of this book as a resource for your classroom is an indicator that you suspect a child in your class has a disability or has already been identified with a specific disability. Perhaps a child in your classroom appears to be developing at a different rate than the other children in the classroom or a child may be exhibiting behaviors that concern you.

This book is designed to help you teach children who have special needs. The following chapters will help you identify characteristics of children with special needs and describe specific strategies you can use as you teach all of the children in your classroom. Although making a diagnosis is not within the framework of our effort, we have included basic information about disabilities that may assist you in approaching curriculum development and lesson planning with appropriate classroom strategies to meet the learning needs of all learners. Please note that this book is not all-inclusive and that additional resources are listed to help you obtain more information on specific subjects.

Chapters 3–10 begin with a scenario that describes how a child with a specific special need might behave in the classroom. Although the scenarios depict real children, it is important to understand that each child in your classroom is unique and the characteristics of the children described reflect only some manifestations of the disability. The disabilities we focus on in this book include autism spectrum disorder, attention deficit/hyperactivity disorder (ADHD), speech and language impairments, hearing impairments, vision impairments, orthopedic impairments, developmental delay, and traumatic brain injury.

Table 1 defines the most notable characteristics that children with various disabilities will demonstrate. Again, each child is unique and will possess specific needs and strengths. This table serves as a general overview of the various disabilities with which children in your classroom may be identified.

As we mentioned previously, Chapters 3–10 of this book begin with a scenario that describes how one specific child might behave in the classroom. These scenarios may help you to understand the child's disability as you might experience it in your classroom. Following each scenario is an overview of the disability. A second section entitled "What Teachers Need to Know About Children With . . ." goes into more detail about the specific disability. This added information also will be useful for families

Table 1

COMMON CHARACTERISTICS OF CHILDREN WITH SPECIFIC SPECIAL NEEDS

Special Need	Characteristics
Children With Autism Spectrum Disorder	• Develop language differently than most children (most often delayed) • Experience minimum social development (not spontaneous) • Often participate in repetitive behaviors (such as echolalia, the repetition of sounds) • Often exhibit disruptive behavior (especially in classrooms) • Are highly sensitive to sensory experiences and movement • Demonstrate irregular intellectual development (unusual patterns of strengths and weaknesses)
Children With Attention Deficit/ Hyperactivity Disorder (ADHD)	• Show inattentive behavior • Exhibit hyperactive and impulsive behaviors • Experience difficulty in relationships with adults and peers • Often have low self-esteem
Children With Speech and/ or Language Impairments	• Possess disorders that affect the rate and rhythm of speech • Often cannot produce various sounds • Often omit or add sounds when producing words • Often distort sounds • May have voice disorders, such as an unusually high pitch or nasality (when sounds seem to be emitted through children's noses) • May possess limited ability to express themselves (language impairment) • May experience difficulty following directions or understanding verbal emotions (language impairment)
Children With Hearing Impairments	• Often ignore adults and/or peers when they are spoken to • May exhibit confusion when responding to questions or instructions • Often cannot hear unless they are facing the speaker • Often demonstrate unclear language production • Often struggle with social behaviors • May be unable to hear in a noisy classroom (sensory defensiveness)
Children With Vision Impairments	• Have impairments ranging from minor deficits to total blindness • May experience different levels of eye function from day to day • Are visually affected by classroom lighting, time of day, and weather • May be hypersensitive to touch (tactile defensiveness) • May have other disabilities (up to 60% of children with visual impairments do) • Tend to rely on nonverbal senses to receive information
Children With Orthopedic Impairments (Physical Impairments)	• May have a congenital condition • May have cerebral palsy, spina bifida, muscular dystrophy, and/or fractures or burns; orthopedic impairments vary widely depending on the specific type of orthopedic impairment (congenital conditions or as a result of accidents) • May experience paralysis, tightness or weakness in the legs or throughout the body, or chronic inflammation and pain of the joints • May or may not have a learning disability
Children With Developmental Delays	• Acquire skills and knowledge at a delayed rate • May have problems with hearing and vision • Have difficulty attending to classroom activities • Might be a result of environmental factors • Have delayed language development
Children With Traumatic Brain Injury	• May have experienced an external physical injury • Have difficulty gaining educational achievement • May exhibit motor dysfunction • Often have problems with attention and memory • May have difficulties in communicating with others • May exhibit social and emotional changes

in their own conceptualization of their child's unique development. You may want to share these sections with individual families or perhaps with all of the families in your classroom. The next section in these chapters describes classroom strategies that may be implemented with children who have special needs. Each strategy will be defined along with one or two classroom accounts demonstrating how the strategy is utilized with individual children.

Finally, three important chapters provide tips on how to collaborate with families, a summary of federal laws that impact practice in preschool centers and public schools, and how to adapt classroom materials to meet the needs of all learners. Not only will we share information for families with children who have special needs, but we will discuss various strategies that can be used to share information about children with special needs with the families of other children in the classroom.

Primarily, this book defines inclusive classrooms and what teachers should know in order to work with children with disabilities within the inclusive setting. A more thorough description of inclusive classrooms follows in Chapter 2, but the following list is an overview of characteristics that should be found in inclusive classrooms:

- Inclusive classrooms have at least one child with a special need. In preschool classrooms, children with special needs are not always identified.
- The inclusive classroom should not have more than 10% of its students identified as having special needs.
- Teachers in inclusive classrooms should have a strong background in child development principles and recognize that development occurs over time and is different for every child. Consequently, teachers should continually assess various aspects of the inclusive classroom. This includes making decisions about room arrangement, reviewing classroom instruction, and working with families, as well as assessing children's developmental progress to maximize each child's learning potential.
- Teachers organize instruction in order to meet children's needs as a group and as individuals. When instructing the group, teachers adjust their plans to accommodate for any child with a disability.
- Teachers plan instruction so that children, regardless of their development, will have activities that provide opportunities for them to develop confidence and competence in learning as well

as experience appropriate challenges. The design of appropriate and inclusive learning experiences helps children feel good about what they are learning, but also challenges them to move to higher levels of knowledge acquisition.

- Teachers document learning for all children in the classroom using assessment strategies that meet the needs of the children's ages, individual needs, and growth.
- Inclusive classrooms maintain regular contact with families and service providers (such as speech therapists, intervention specialists, and other professionals who work with children with special needs).
- Children in inclusive classrooms learn together regardless of their differences and abilities. Their opportunities to interact give all children invaluable experiences with others who may learn or interact in different ways.
- Inclusive classrooms are a microcosm of the larger society. When children with special needs enter classrooms, they are given the chance to adjust to real-world activities that they will need to understand when they become adults. Likewise, young children learn to accept others who are different and develop respect for all children.

Successful Inclusion Strategies for Early Childhood Teachers is a practical guide for working with children who have special learning needs. Teachers and caregivers who love working with young children are aware that teaching is a profession that poses challenges, as well as emotional rewards, to those who want the best for children. Our hope is that this book will capitalize on your desire to be the best teacher for *all* of the children in your classroom.

CHAPTER

1

Overview of Disability Laws That Affect Inclusive Classrooms

F or the past 50 years, the federal government has developed laws that affect classroom practice, beginning with the Elementary and Secondary Education Act of 1965. It is helpful for teachers and childcare providers to know and understand these laws, as federal law mandates that schools and childcare centers serve children with special needs appropriately. National interest in children with special needs began in the early 1970s with the enactment of the Rehabilitation Act of 1973, a Civil Rights law that prohibits discrimination on the basis of disabilities in public and private programs receiving federal funds. Today this legal provision is more commonly known as Section 504.

The most significant legislative action that affected children with disabilities passed in 1975 with the Education for All Handicapped Children Act. The Americans with Disabilities Act (ADA) was passed in 1990. That same year, the Education for All Handicapped Children Act was reauthorized as the Individuals with Disabilities Education Act, more commonly known as IDEA. IDEA was renamed in 1997 and reauthorized in 2004 (effective July 1, 2005).

The 1983 amendments to the Education for All Handicapped Children Act required preschool children with disabilities (ages 3–5) to receive services. In addition, a grant program was established to assist states in their development of a comprehensive system of early intervention services for infants and toddlers as well as their families. All of these laws require public schools and childcare centers, as well as Head Start programs, to develop procedures for identifying children with special needs, provide individual assessments for diagnosis of children, and develop an Individualized Education Program (IEP; ages 3–21) or Individualized Family Service Plan (IFSP; ages birth to 3) for the child's education. Early intervention services were defined by the 1997 update to IDEA. The following discussion clarifies how ADA and IDEA affect childcare centers and Head Start programs and how intervention services impact children and their families.

AMERICANS WITH DISABILITIES ACT (ADA)

Most American adults have seen the impact of the Americans with Disabilities Act on their lives, as communities have had to restructure streets and sidewalks to accommodate people with disabilities. Public buildings and restrooms are required to be accessible for all citizens, and informational signs must provide signage in Braille for individuals who are blind. The ADA also mandated equal access to jobs and education. Not only does this law require compliance in all American communities, but childcare centers and Head Start programs also must comply with this law (see the section titled "Questions About the Americans with Disabilities Act and Childcare Centers" on pp. 13–15 in this chapter). ADA specified that childcare centers and family or home daycare programs are included in the definition of public accommodations that must adhere to this law. In addition, childcare centers are required to make reasonable modifications to their procedures and policies to accommodate adults and children with disabilities. For example, "This may mean that centers that do not normally accept children who are not yet toilet trained may have to make accommodations to do so if a disability is an obstacle to the toilet training" (Cook, Klein, & Tessier, 2008, p. 15). In addition, if children or adults with hearing, vision, or speech disabilities need auxiliary aids and services to ensure communication, a center must provide these.

INDIVIDUALS WITH DISABILITIES EDUCATION ACT (IDEA)

When the Education for All Handicapped Children Act was enacted in 1975, it defined categories of disability as mental retardation (MR); emotional disturbance (ED); learning disabilities (LD); impairments in vision, hearing, speech, or language; deafness; blindness; orthopedic and other health impairments; and multiple disabilities. The Individuals with Disabilities Education Act added autism and traumatic brain injuries to the list in 1990 and provided funding to improve services to infants and young children. Children with these disabilities are defined later in this chapter in the section titled "General Characteristics of Children With Special Needs" (see pp. 5–8).

The IDEA amendments of 1997 ensured access for children ages 3–21 years old (Part B) and for children birth to age 2 (part C) to inclusive environments. This federal enactment shows a clear preference for inclusive classrooms as the appropriate delivery system for children with special needs (Smith & Rapport, 1999). Part C states that "early intervention services for children from birth to age 3 are to be provided in natural environments, including the home, and community settings in which children without disabilities participate" (IDEA, 1997).

THE EARLY INTERVENTION PROGRAM FOR INFANTS AND TODDLERS WITH DISABILITIES

IDEA (1997) required public school systems to work with families whose young children have disabilities and are about to enter preschool programs. This law emphasized the need to provide for early intervention services in children's natural environments, which include their homes and community settings, such as childcare centers or any setting that would serve children's typically developing peers of the same age.

> Each child's individual plan must state the degree to which the child will receive services in "natural environments." Natural environments include not only the child's home but also neighborhood play groups, child development centers, Head Start programs, and any other setting designed for children without disabilities. (Cook et al., 2008, p. 16)

Because this statute requires states to develop policies to comply with the law, services vary from state to state. Most programs provide assistance with strategies for families to work with their young children and the development of Individualized Family Service Plans (IFSPs; Warner & Sower, 2005).

Clarification of IDEA Part B relates to children between the ages of 3 and 21 through special education services; IDEA Part C relates directly to children from birth to 2 for early invention. Most early (birth to 2) diagnoses are done by pediatricians; the services they receive for intervention are usually done in the home or hospital setting, coordinated through the pediatrician and outside agencies. Children ages 3 to 21 usually are serviced in an educational setting, based on the IFSP/IEP team decision as to the least restrictive environment (LRE) for the child. These intervention meetings take place at least every year. Families are able to call a meeting anytime they have questions about their child's services or progress. Families who are concerned about their child's development should consult the child's pediatrician or the local school district's Department of Special Education for specific instructions on how to initiate a full evaluation.

The 1990 reauthorization of the Education for All Handicapped Children Act expanded the statute to define 13 disability terms. The 13 terms include: autism, deaf-blindness, deafness, emotional disturbance, hearing impairment, mental retardation, multiple disabilities, orthopedic impairment, other health impairment, specific learning disability, speech or language impairment, traumatic brain injury, and visual impairment (including partial sight and blindness). IDEA (2004) clearly articulated that a specific learning disability (SLD) does not include learning problems that are a primary result of mental retardation or visual, hearing, or motor disabilities. In addition, SLD does not include learning problems that are a primary result of emotional disturbance or of cultural, economic, or environmental disadvantage.

In addition, IDEA has addressed ADHD in its definition of other health impairment (OHI). Specifically, IDEA (2004) specified that OHI is due to chronic or acute health problems such as asthma, ADHD, epilepsy, heart conditions, lead poisoning, and other specific health problems.

GENERAL CHARACTERISTICS OF CHILDREN WITH SPECIAL NEEDS

Children with special needs often are lumped into one "disability category" without consideration of the type of need they may have. Children with special needs who are more commonly placed in inclusive early childhood classrooms often are placed in a broad category of higher incidence disabilities. Such disabilities include speech and language impairments, specific learning disabilities, emotional disturbance, and mental retardation (also referred to as intellectual disability and/or developmental delay). The degree of severity of each disability may vary from mild to more severe in nature. Children with lower incidence disabilities such as visual impairments, hearing impairments, orthopedic impairments, autism, other health impairments, and severe multiple impairments, are served less often in childcare settings. However, in recent years, the number of children with lower incidence disabilities, particularity autism, in early childhood classrooms has been rising.

Although IDEA (2004) defined 13 specific disabilities, the special needs categories defined in this book differ slightly from those addressed in IDEA and are as follows: autism spectrum disorder, speech and language impairments, attention deficit/hyperactivity disorder (ADHD), hearing impairment, vision impairment, orthopedic impairment, and cognitive and/or developmental delay (intellectual disabilities). For preschoolers, learning disabilities (as defined by IDEA [2004]), when diagnosed, typically fall into the areas of listening comprehension and oral expression. For information on addressing these issues, the reader can refer to Chapter 5 on speech and language impairments (pp. 77–95).

Autism Spectrum Disorder

In recent years, the number of children diagnosed with autism spectrum disorders has increased, and, thus, more children with autism are being enrolled in early childhood classrooms. Autism is classified as a developmental disability, generally becoming evident before the age of 3. Children with autism typically have difficulty in communication and social interactions. They frequently demonstrate repetitive motor behaviors, such as rocking or hand weaving. It is important to note that a spectrum of behaviors exist in children diagnosed with ASD. More specifically, children with ASD have skills that range from higher functioning to lower functioning.

Speech and/or Language Impairments

Children with speech and/or language impairments commonly are educated in inclusive classrooms. Children with such impairments tend to have problems in communication and possibly in oral motor functions. Children with speech and language disorders may have speech impairments related specifically to the proper enunciation of specific sounds (articulation disorders) or language impairments that involve syntax or semantic errors in speech. Language disorders also may involve delayed language or receptive language impairments.

Attention Deficit/Hyperactivity Disorder

In IDEA (2004), other health impairment (OHI) refers to significant limitations in strength, vitality, or alertness that affect a child's learning. OHI can be the result of asthma, heart problems, diabetes, or other health issues, and includes children diagnosed with Attention Deficit/Hyperactivity Disorder. A physician or psychologist diagnoses ADHD. This diagnosis includes children with serious problems with overactivity or attention, or both. The diagnosis may result in children who take daily oral medications to control their impulsive behavior. Although IDEA (2004) did not recognize ADHD as a disability category, it did mention ADHD in the definition of other health impairment, and most schools provide services to children with ADHD under this category.

Hearing Impairment

A hearing impairment is an impairment in hearing that negatively affects a child's educational performance. This impairment would not be so severe that a child could not hear speech and environmental sounds in the classroom when wearing a hearing aid. If the child cannot hear speech or environmental sounds, even with the help of a hearing aid, then the child would be identified as deaf (lacking residual hearing).

Vision Impairment

Another sensory impairment addressed in this book is vision impairment. Children with visual impairments are identified as those children who, even with correction (e.g., glasses or contacts), experience limited vision that adversely affects their educational experience.

Orthopedic Impairment

Orthopedic impairment means an impairment due to congenital irregularities (e.g., a clubfoot, spina bifida, missing or ill-formed limb), impairments due to the effects of disease (e.g., polio or bone tuberculosis), and impairments from other causes (e.g., cerebral palsy or amputations). Severe orthopedic impairments often adversely affect children's educational performances.

Cognitive and/or Developmental Delay

The National Dissemination Center for Children with Disabilities (NICHCY, 2004b) defined intellectual disabilities as a term used to describe

> when a person has certain limitations in mental functioning and in skills such as communicating, taking care of himself or herself, and social skills. These limitations will cause a child to learn and develop more slowly than a typical child. Children with cognitive disabilities may take longer to learn to speak, walk, and take care of their personal needs such as dressing or eating. (para. 3)

Cognitive or intellectual disabilities may or may not coexist with other specific disabilities such as speech and language impairment, a hearing impairment, or other health impairments. IDEA (1997) provided provisions that permit the use of the category *developmental delay* to be applied to children ages birth through 9 for purposes of qualifying for special education services under IDEA. The Division for Early Childhood (DEC) of the Council for Exceptional Children (2005) defined developmental delay as a condition which represents a significant delay in the process of development. It does not refer to a condition in which a child is slightly or momentarily lagging in development. The presence of developmental delay is an indication that the process of development is significantly affected and that without special intervention, it is likely that educational performance at school age will be affected. (p. 1)

Within the context of this book, we use the term developmental delay rather than mental retardation, intellectual disability, or cognitive disability because this terminology is more commonly accepted by professionals in the field of early childhood special education and more appropriate for children identified from birth through age 9. See Appendix A for the DEC Position Statement on "Developmental Delay as an Eligibility Category." (Note that DEC prefers use of developmental delay through age 8.)

Traumatic Brain Injury

Traumatic brain injury (TBI) is an injury to the brain, usually caused by an external physical force to the head. The result is total or partial brain functioning that adversely affects a child's educational performance. The disability results in impairments in one or more areas, such as cognition; language; memory; attention; reasoning; abstract thinking; judgment; problem solving; sensory, perceptual, and motor abilities; psychosocial behavior; physical functions; information processing; and speech. The term does not apply to brain injuries that are congenital.

For additional information, the National Dissemination Center for Children with Disabilities—a leading source of information and resources for families, caregivers, educators, and other professionals in the field of special education—has developed a complete resource list and fact sheet on each of the above mentioned disabilities. Fact sheets, parent and family resources, and teaching tips are available on its Web site (http://www.nichcy.org).

HOW FEDERAL LAWS AFFECT EARLY CHILDHOOD CLASSROOMS

The laws that support children with special needs affect all early childhood classrooms from childcare centers, to Head Start programs, to public school systems. The legislation implies that personnel in early childhood classrooms—administrators and teachers alike—must understand and implement all laws. Recently, legislation has recommended the use of inclusive classrooms, and recognition of various inclusion models is imperative in early childhood settings. Early childhood educators should be aware of the following expectations:

1. *Know the laws that govern classrooms for children with special needs.* The Individuals with Disabilities Education Act prescribes least restrictive environments (LRE) and "natural environments" in the home and community for children with special needs. LREs and natural environments are classrooms in which typically developing, same-age peers are educated. The intent of these laws is to assist children with special needs in receiving an education equal to that of their peers without disabilities.

2. *Deny no child admission.* When families bring their children with disabilities to a childcare center, Head Start program, or public school setting, the centers and programs must enroll those children. No one can deny a child's entrance to the early childhood program, except in two conditions: when the child displays a direct threat to other children, or if the program would have to be seriously altered to accept the child. All teachers, regardless of their educational backgrounds, must be prepared to work with children who have special needs, and centers are required to develop assessment procedures to determine whether children may be admitted. Center policies also must reflect procedures that promote inclusion in their classrooms. Paraprofessionals may be available to help classroom teachers with children who have severe disabilities, but the least restrictive environment for children with special needs is the classroom in which typically developing, same-age peers are educated.

3. *Be prepared to work with children with special needs.* Teachers are required to work with children who have special needs. Therefore, they need information about basic educational strategies that work with all children. Personnel in early childhood

classrooms must attend workshops to receive training about working with children who may have autism, ADHD, or any number of impairments that affect children's performance in classrooms. Using evidence-based practice is the backbone to every child's educational experience, and children with disabilities have unique needs that require specialized training on the part of the adults who work with them. Additionally, all people who work with children who have disabilities need to reflect on their attitudes toward children with special needs.

4. *Understand the importance of school/family partnerships.* Children with special needs have families who love them and care for them, as do families of typically developing children. Their families often are well educated about the laws affecting their children's education, and they most often have an abundance of knowledge about how their children should be educated. When children with special needs arrive at the classroom door, be prepared to listen carefully to families' concerns and the information they have about educating their children. They know the special issues that their children have. The relationship educators form with families will facilitate the transition children will need to adjust to the classroom setting. For further discussion of this partnership, please refer to Chapter 11 of this book.

5. *When necessary, work with other professionals to meet the needs of individual children and their families.* Occasionally, children with special needs have needs that require them to have additional assistance from other professionals in the community. Speech and language pathologists, physical therapists, or other service providers might come to the classroom at a scheduled time to work with individual children or children might leave the classroom at an appointed time to have instruction for their specific disability. How children and families interact with other professionals depends on the preschool inclusion model the school is using and/or the IEP or IFSP that has been developed for the family.

6. *Be aware of community resources available when families need assistance.* Community resources available to families who have children with disabilities vary from state to state because of the development of special education laws, especially the Early

Intervention Program for Infants and Toddlers with Disabilities (part of the Education for All Handicapped Children Act). They also vary from community to community because of funding sources. Consult your local public school's special education director for the most accurate information about resources available to children with disabilities in your classroom.

7. *Be an advocate for children with special needs.* Sometimes, the role of advocate is thrust upon early childhood educators because they become the first person to talk to other families about specific children with disabilities enrolled in their classrooms (see Chapter 12 for tips about talking to other families who ask questions about children with disabilities). Educators also can become advocates in the community and with legislators, especially as they begin to understand the reason why laws exist that protect and support children with disabilities. As a society, we need to learn how to support all members of our citizenry. In doing so, we strengthen the entire nation and become more supportive to all around us.

EARLY CHILDHOOD SPECIAL EDUCATION SETTINGS

Early childhood special education services are provided in multiple settings. Most frequently, services are identified as either home-based or center-based programs. Specific therapies or interventions are provided in each of the above settings in accordance to the child's IFSP or IEP. Often children younger than 2 or those who have significant or multiple disabilities are served in the home-based setting. In this setting, an emphasis is often placed on "having professional staff teach parents how to most effectively meet their children's needs. In addition, home based programs are child-oriented and emphasize having professionals provide direct intervention services" (Dunlap, 2008, p. 69). In addition, these programs are required by law to be family oriented. More information on working with families can be found in Chapter 12.

In the center-based program, children receive interventions or services in the daycare setting or preschool. Often, specific therapies are included within the context of the child's regular day. For example, daily speech therapy might be provided during Circle Time or when adults and children are interacting. Center-based services vary greatly from a self-contained classroom (designed for children with disabilities) to a more inclusive setting where services are provided in the classroom in which typically developing peers are instructed. When services cannot be provided within the classroom setting in the center-based program, children with special needs may be served during a pull-out session (e.g., temporarily taken to another room to receive therapy or services such as occupational therapy [OT] or physical therapy [PT]).

Regardless of the type of services a child receives, "there are several key attributes of effective intervention programs, including the use of DAP's designed to meet each child's individual needs in culturally sensitive, inclusive, and play oriented ways" (Dunlap, 2008, p. 87). DAPs, or developmentally appropriate practices, combine child development theories with information on the individual child to create effective programming.

PRESCHOOL INCLUSION MODELS

Preschool inclusion models form organizational contexts for preschool inclusion. Wolery and Odom (2000) and Odom et al. (1999) defined three basic structures found in the United States: (1) community-based childcare, (2) Head Start, and (3) public school programs. As mentioned earlier in this chapter, inclusion models are defined by individual state policies and procedures and are dependent on funding provided by national and state governmental agencies. The three structures are recognized in the following forms.

Community-Based Childcare

Community-based childcare programs are childcare programs that individual local proprietors or community organizations own and operate. They include for-profit national programs (often referred to as corporate childcare), local church or community mother's day out programs, and nonprofit preschools for children from low-income families. The Americans with Disabilities Act requires these programs to accept children with disabilities.

Head Start

Community agencies, as well as regional Head Start programs, fall into this category. Local Head Start agencies are operated by community agencies and typically are housed in a local facility or school district building. Head Start programs are required to provide inclusion classrooms for children with special needs.

Public School Programs

Public school preschool programs often are available for educationally at-risk children and often are funded by Title I funds. Other entities classified in this category are public school Head Start programs, special education classes that include children without disabilities, and tuition-based childcare programs.

Regardless of the inclusion model, the critical features for early childhood professionals are teacher training and teacher attitudes toward children who have special needs. For more information about each of these organizational structures and the benefits and challenges of each, see http://www.fpg.unc.edu/~publicationsoffice/pdfs/AdmGuide.pdf.

QUESTIONS ABOUT THE AMERICANS WITH DISABILITIES ACT AND CHILDCARE CENTERS

A document called "Commonly Asked Questions About Child Care Centers and the Americans with Disabilities Act" is available from the U.S. Department of Justice at http://www.usdoj.gov/crt/ada/childq%26a.htm. The following describes some of the more frequently asked questions and their answers, but other questions of interest are online for interested early childhood educators.

- *Does ADA apply to childcare centers?* Yes. Both privately owned childcare centers and services provided by government agencies must comply with the law. You may call the ADA Information Line for answers to technical questions about the law at 800-514-0301 (voice) or 800-514-0383 (TDD). Technical assistance materials also are available for individuals to order.

- *How do I determine whether a child with a disability belongs in my program?* Centers must develop individualized assessment procedures to determine whether their program can accommodate the needs of specific children with disabilities. The law allows centers to deny access to children who might impose a direct threat to others in the program or who might fundamentally alter the nature of the program. The law does not require providers to take children with disabilities out of turn if there is a waiting list for entrance.

- *When a child needs individualized attention and our center specializes in group childcare, can we deny access to our program?* No. All children require individualized attention occasionally, and excluding a child who needs one-on-one care violates the law.

- *What about a child who bites? Are we required to keep the child in our center, even when the child has a disability?* The first action is to work with families to see if there is a way to curb the child's negative behavior. If the child continues to pose a direct threat, the child may be removed from the program.

- *Do we have to enroll a child who has a seeing-eye dog when we have an explicit "no pets" policy?* Yes. The seeing-eye dog is a service animal, not a pet. Consider revising your "no pets" policy to allow an exception for service animals.

- *Our center also has a policy that states that we will not give medication to any child. What should we do for a child who requires medication in order to function within the group?* According to law, reasonable care should be taken in following doctors' and families' written instructions about administering medications to children who need it for access to the program. Consult professionals in your state about liability issues surrounding this question.

- *Our center has a policy that we will not accept children more than 3 years of age who need diapering. If a child older than 3 with a disability that requires diapering requests entrance into our program, can we deny access?* Generally, the answer is no. Children who need diapering because of a disability cannot be denied. Personnel should not be required to leave other children in order to diaper any child.

- *Can we exclude children with HIV or AIDS in order to protect other children and our employees?* No, centers cannot exclude a child solely because that child has HIV or AIDS. Centers must require their employees to use universally accepted precautions (such as the use of latex gloves) when they are cleaning or bandaging children who are wounded or bleeding.

- *Do we have to enroll children who have life-threatening allergies (to bee stings or specific foods)?* Generally, the answer is yes. Personnel should be prepared to take appropriate action if a child has a medical emergency (such as administering medication provided by families or guardians).

- *Am I required by law to make my childcare center's building, playground, and parking lot accessible to people with disabilities when I do not have a child with special needs in my program?* Yes. Barriers to access by people with disabilities must be removed if the renovation can be accomplished easily and without much expense. Buildings constructed after January 1993 must comply strictly with ADA Standards for Accessible Design.

- *Has the Department of Justice ever sued a childcare provider for ADA violations?* Yes. Lawsuits have been filed against childcare providers for refusing to enroll a 4-year-old child with HIV, and the Department of Justice has participated as a "friend of the court" against a center for not allowing a child with multiple disabilities to attend its program.

In addition, the Americans with Disabilities Act Web site is updated frequently and contains regulations, press releases, and technical assistance materials for early childhood professionals. The site is available at http://www.ada.gov for those who are interested.

IF YOU WANT TO KNOW MORE

National Dissemination Center for Children With Disabilities
http://www.nichcy.org

An Administrator's Guide to Preschool Inclusion
http://www.fpg.unc.edu/~publicationsoffice/pdfs/AdmGuide.pdf

Commonly Asked Questions About Child Care Centers and the Americans With Disabilities Act
http://www.usdoj.gov/crt/ada/childq%26a.htm

ADA Home Page
http://www.ada.gov

CHAPTER 2

What Is an Inclusive Classroom?

As you walk through the hallways at Little Learners Early Learning Center it appears to be a typical childcare facility. Peeking into the 3-year-old classroom, you can see many children engaged in play activities throughout the learning centers. Maria is dressed up as "mommy" and Kylie is covering her drawing paper with long strands of yarn and pompoms. Standing at the door, you can hear the laughter coming from the classroom next door where all of the 2-year-olds are wearing pink piggy ears and retelling the story of "The Three Little Pigs." Each child seems to be enjoying his or her time at school. Of course, there are days when a child might not follow directions or days when tears are streaming down someone's face because he or she fell down or lost his or her favorite toy. But today, this is not the case. Today is one of those days that directors love and one of those days when teachers restock their patience and rekindle their love for teaching.

So, what makes this preschool different? What makes it special? What makes this preschool stand out from the rest? The answer is simple: It is what you don't see. You don't see children that have the same needs or life experiences. You don't see children with special needs turned away at the door or frowned upon when registering. You don't see discrimination or segregation within the classrooms, and you don't walk into a classroom and think to yourself "that child must have special needs."

The focus at this preschool is inclusion, a model that has changed the way that all children are taught, a model that supports, welcomes, and encourages diversity. It is a school where teachers have embraced challenges and learned to enhance the learning environment to meet the needs of children with special needs and their families. It is one of the many preschools in our country that have taken a leap forward to provide quality care and education for all children, regardless of whether or not they have a specific special need.

SO, WHAT IS INCLUSION?

A great deal of debate has occurred over the adoption of a single definition of inclusion. However, for the sake of this book, inclusion for preschoolers will be defined as placing children with disabilities into classes with typically developing peers, as appropriate, and providing them with the necessary services and supports to enable them to benefit from being there (Rafferty, 2002). Including preschool children with special needs in childcare and public school facilities has become common practice in today's society.

However, the degree to which children are included varies from facility to facility. The actual practice of including all children comes with benefits and challenges for both children with special needs and their typically developing peers. Addressing these challenges and embracing the benefits occur only when caregivers truly understand the rationale and impact that inclusion has on the structure of their classrooms.

Including a child with special needs involves more than just accepting a child into your classroom. It involves understanding that child's special needs and how they impact not only the way that child learns and plays with other children in the classroom, but also his or her typically developing peers in the classroom. If a program places a child with special needs in a classroom setting with typically developing peers, yet that child does not interact with the other children or is physically separated from them during activities and lessons, then the justification for inclusion does not exist.

Inclusion cannot be thought of as a place, but rather the practice of fully enabling all children to participate actively in that environment. In order to achieve this, additional assistance may be required for a child with special needs.

WHY INCLUSION?

Many children with special needs are receiving their education in inclusive childcare facilities. The reasons specific centers choose to support preschool inclusion vary. However, all childcare directors and caregivers should be aware of the federal laws about inclusion. Section 504 of the Rehabilitation Act of 1973, the Americans with Disabilities Act, and the Individuals with Disabilities Education Act are the federal laws that have a direct impact on inclusive practices. Detailed descriptions of each law are available in Chapter 1 of this book. In addition, many states have had class action suits filed in regards to inclusive practices of 3- to 5-year-olds. Inclusion is not just a legal mandate; there also are many benefits for children with and without special needs.

Recently, the Council for Exceptional Children's Division of Early Childhood (DEC) and the National Association for the Education of Young Children (NAEYC) published a joint position statement on inclusion. This statement can be found in Appendix B and accessed online at the DEC Web site (http://www.dec-sped.org/About_DEC/PositionConcept_Papers/Inclusion). The statement clearly identified the need for inclusive practices and addresses developmentally appropriate practices within the inclusive setting.

EXAMINING THE BENEFITS OF INCLUSION

When asking caregivers in inclusive setting why they have chosen to include children with special needs into their centers, the answers range from "it is ethically right and we are legally bound" to "all children gain and learn so much when they are together." There is no doubt that including all children, regardless of their special needs, presents challenges; however, when done correctly, it is evident that many benefits exist. Children with special needs, typically developing peers, families of all children, and childcare providers directly benefit from inclusive practices.

Children with special needs gain a great deal through socialization with typically developing peers. Their peers are able to model appropriate social interactions for them and provide the opportunity for participation in such interactions. For example, a child with a special need may not interact the same way with a toy as a typically developing child. The interaction may not be systematic. However, when a typically developing peer models and engages the child with special needs in play, the child with special needs is more likely to observe the proper way to interact with the toy in a more meaningful way.

Early childhood educational environments are locations where children observe and develop social behaviors as well as gross motor, fine motor, and communication skills. Through these social interactions, children with special needs are able to form friendships with peers, and often these relationships are the ones that help a child to establish feelings of self-worth and acceptance as a member of the learning community.

Children with special needs are not the only ones benefiting from the social interactions occurring in inclusive classrooms. Inclusion affords typically developing peers the opportunity to establish new and diverse friendships. In addition, they gain the awareness of special needs and diversity that children in a noninclusive setting often may not value. Many caregivers report that children without special needs who spend time in inclusive settings develop a strong sense of their own strengths while at the same time recognize the abilities of children with special needs in their classrooms. Many times, situations arise that help reinforce the concepts of respect, patience, and responsibility.

Inclusive settings also provide the parents and family members of all children with opportunities to learn. Parents and family members of children with special needs may be hesitant to place their children into this setting. The same holds true for the parent or family member of the typically developing child. The opportunities to support each other in this endeavor are numerous. Such support decreases feelings of isolation and self-doubt while promoting feelings of confidence.

ADDRESSING CHALLENGES

As previously mentioned, the actual practice of including all children comes with benefits as well as challenges. Addressing the challenges and being proactive in your approach is imperative for a program to be successful. The challenges caregivers often cite include overcoming parental fears, dealing with inappropriate behaviors within the classroom, struggling to accommodate or adapt the curriculum, and an inability to create a feeling of community within the classroom. First and foremost, it is important for caregivers to know that these concerns are valid and common. Second, caregivers often must recognize that they will have to cross over a few bridges before reaching the final destination. Carefully examining concerns and then developing a plan of action for addressing the concerns is the first step that caregivers and administrators must take in childcare facilities.

Family Concerns

Families of both children with special needs and their typically developing peers may express fears and worry about the safety and academic needs of their children. Developing open lines of communication between families is the key to overcoming this common challenge. Instead of taking a critical approach and devaluing their concerns, caregivers should listen and openly address the fears they may have.

For example, if a parent or family member expresses a fear that his or her child may be teased due to the child's specific special need, caregivers should explain how they will structure the lessons and what accommodations they will make to assure that the child will become an active member of the classroom. This is a time when family members need reassurance that the caregiver will build on the child's strengths to help the child find his place in the classroom.

If a parent or family member questions how the school or center might handle the concerns of those families of typically developing children who do not support inclusion, caregivers should be prepared with a reply that is honest but does not avoid the reality of the situation. It is important that families understand that not everyone accepts and supports inclusive early childhood educational settings.

A teacher or childcare administrator cannot control the thoughts a child's parent or family member might have, or what that family member does. This should be made clear to each family member. Be direct, and remind the families of the laws supporting inclusion. Tell them that you will share with the families of the children in the class the benefits that an inclusive classroom will have on their child.

Another factor that has been identified by families as a concern regarding inclusion is the barrier of the physical environment. Parents of children with specific disabilities may express concerns regarding access to the building or classrooms via ramps or may question the width of doorways, exit areas, or restroom facilities. In most cases, this problem easily can be addressed by assuring families that the facility itself is ADA compliant and that specific accommodations can be made to overcome any physical limitations that their child may have that could impact his ability to successfully navigate the environment.

Professionals' Concerns

Parents are not alone in being concerned about including all children in the classroom. You may question your own abilities about working with children with special needs. Often, this concern comes from a lack of understanding about responsibilities or a lack of prior experiences in adapting and modifying curriculum for children with special needs. One of the greatest challenges faced in providing an inclusive early childhood program is that the amount of training and understanding of the needs of children with disabilities is varied. This, along with differences in philosophical views of teachers and staff, can cause unique challenges to you as a teacher.

If you have these fears, you should discuss them with your director or principal. In order for inclusion of young children to be successful, the administration needs to be aware that many teachers are unprepared to work with children with diverse needs. Additional support and professional development may be necessary. This book can be useful as a resource and foundation for professional development or as a reference to specific situations as they arise.

In order to prepare for a child with special needs to join your classroom, it is important to learn about the characteristics of the child's special needs. A brief overview of each of the special needs addressed throughout this book is available in Table 1 (see p. xiii). However, it is most important to learn about each child. Ask questions about the strengths the child will bring to the classroom, what specific health needs the child has, as well as what the child's likes and dislikes are. This information will prove helpful in creating an environment that meets the child's social, physical, and developmental needs. With a clear understanding of the child's specific needs, you can begin to examine why instruction is given, the intended outcomes of the lessons, and the physical learning environment. Additionally, you can determine if a child with special needs can participate in the activity without having to provide any additional modifications or adaptations.

Adapting and/or modifying the curriculum will depend in a large part on the specific special need a child has and the level of support the child may need to reach the intended outcome of the lesson. Each chapter of this book will address the specific ways to adapt the curriculum based on the child's needs. However, a general rule caregivers everywhere should follow in determining the level of support a child will need or the degree to which to modify a lesson is to base decisions on the answers to the following questions:

- Can the child participate in the activity . . .
    - as it currently is planned?
    - if you change the way you present it to the children?
    - if you adapt the materials?
    - if you have an additional support person?
    - if you adapt the evaluation criteria or overall goal?

Asking these questions will help determine the need for and level of support that the child may require to be a successful participant in the inclusive classroom setting. It is possible to provide a greater level of support than the child needs.

For example, a child with a speech impairment may not need to communicate through sign language. If sign language is not necessary in order for the child to communicate (the child's speech is comprehensible), then the extensive use of sign language throughout the day may cause the child to rely on signing rather than the spoken word. This also can happen if a child who is able to speak is allowed to point when requesting objects rather than using words to request an object.

For some children, you might gradually fade the use of adaptations and accommodations as the child gains skills. The goal of providing adaptations is to help the child fully participate to the greatest extent possible in the activities taking place in the classroom. As children begin to gain more confidence and acquire the skills necessary to perform a task with less support, gradually phase out the support. For example, a child pointing to requested objects should begin to pair the pointing request with the spoken word. As the child's speech becomes clearer, the expectation should be that the child uses more spoken words and eventually discontinues the pointing. Such a development does not happen overnight but is rather a gradual process that is dependent on the individual child's needs. However, be aware that some children will need ongoing adaptations. For example, a child with cerebral palsy that limits his ability to fully use his legs may need to use a walker or wheelchair throughout his lifetime.

An inclusive preschool classroom can and will look very different depending on the way the program is designed. However, children will reap many benefits from attending a school where caregivers have implemented a successful model of inclusion. The teachers of such a program will be amazed at how quickly they are able to set aside their fears and misconceptions and have instead a keen ability to observe, plan, and welcome all children into their classrooms.

PROVIDING SUPPORT IN THE INCLUSIVE SETTING

Often in an inclusive setting, a key individual, frequently referred to as an inclusion support specialist, provides support to students identified as having special needs. The inclusion support specialist typically is not a discipline specific specialist such as a physical therapist, occupational therapist, or speech therapist. The types of activities that inclusion support specialists provide have been summarized by Dunlap (2008) as:

- providing in-service programs and information to staff members regarding specific disability characteristics,
- modeling of specific interventions and teaching strategies,
- conducting observation and assessment of the child in the inclusive setting,
- providing written feedback and open discussion to teachers about the child's development and performance,
- individually working with a child on an as-needed basis to achieve specific goals,
- modeling various techniques of peer training,
- creating or obtaining adaptive equipment, and
- participating in IFSP or IEP meetings and attending regular staff meetings to provide leadership and consultation.

BEST PRACTICES IN INCLUSIVE CLASSROOMS

Early childhood classrooms as well as inclusive early childhood classrooms are unique in comparison to instructing children in the middle and high school years. Much of the instruction in the early childhood classroom is designed with the understanding that children develop at different rates across developmental domains. This is very apparent in young toddlers and infants. In the preschool setting, best practices involve the use of instructional centers, center choices, discovery centers, Circle Time, hands-on experiences, projects, word walls, big books, and individualized instruction. The principles that guide these best practices are:

- Developing topics of study that are relevant to the children you teach
- Allowing children as much choice as possible
- Limiting large-group experiences
- Providing activities that meet the children's developmental needs
- Using centers and center play for child-directed play and instructional purposes
- Developing hands-on activities that allow children to work directly with objects and materials in their environment
- Utilizing individualized instruction as often as possible, and
- Planning activities that offer multi-level challenges for children. (Warner, Lynch, Nabors, & Simpson, 2007, p. 14)

ACCOMMODATIONS AND MODIFICATIONS

As previously mentioned, one of the challenges faced by teachers is understanding when and how to adapt or modify specific activities and materials to meet the needs of all children in the classroom. In Chapter 11, we address adapting materials to meet the needs of all learners. However, in addition to adapting and modifying materials teachers should determine whether or not accommodations or modifications are needed in the classroom environment, curriculum content, or to the mode of instruction and evaluation. Table 2 provides some examples of specific accommodations/modifications that teacher may find useful. Additional recommendations for specific student needs are found in the chapters on specific disabilities.

Regardless of the type of accommodation or modification, general and special educators, including related service personnel, should collaborate and consult on the curriculum content and materials to be used during instruction. In addition, collaboration on the use of instructional

Table 2

EXAMPLES OF CLASSROOM ACCOMMODATIONS/MODIFICATIONS FOR CHILDREN WITH SPECIAL NEEDS

Disability	Classroom Environment	Curriculum Content	Instruction/Evaluation
Autism Spectrum Disorder	• Organize seating arrangements and classroom furniture to meet the needs of all children (maintain the structure of the physical environment as well as instructional environment) • Seat the child near the teacher or peer buddy as necessary (to support the use of peer tutoring) • Include quiet areas in classroom design • Use carpet squares to designate where the child should sit • The natural environment should support social interaction • Evaluate classroom lighting to determine its effect on child • Create a safe environment that offers protection from teasing and bullying	• Plan individual instruction for content knowledge • Review and determine the most appropriate curriculum for the child's needs • Be prepared to provide follow-up instruction • Provide a consistent classroom schedule and structure • Use simple instructions during lessons • Accept children's responses to questions • Enhance curriculum with the inclusion of social stories	• Encourage and reinforce positive behavior as it is exhibited • Monitor instruction and ask for feedback during lessons • Show a sample of the work that is expected from the child • Provide extended "wait time" for responses from the child • Provide self-monitoring checklists (with pictures or photographs) • Provide additional time for the child to complete his or her work • Use concrete objects as much as possible during instruction and evaluation • Evaluate use of instructional technology based on the individual needs of the child
Attention Deficit/ Hyperactivity Disorder (ADHD)	• Organize seating arrangements and classroom furniture to meet the needs of all children • Provide a highly structured environment (e.g., reduce wide open spaces) • Seat the child near the teacher or peer buddy as necessary • Provide soft background music	• Plan individual instruction for content knowledge • Be prepared to provide follow-up instruction • Consider classwide peer tutoring to support curriculum • Medication usage should be considered in curriculum and instructional planning • Avoid changes in routines and structures without offering a warning • Incorporate behavioral interventions including positive reinforcement	• Encourage and reinforce positive behavior as it is exhibited • Use concrete objects as much as possible during instruction and evaluation • Teach self-monitoring strategies

Disability	Classroom Environment	Curriculum Content	Instruction/Evaluation
Speech and Language Impairments	• Organize seating arrangements and classroom furniture to meet the needs of all children • Seat the child near the teacher or peer buddy as necessary • Verbal participation should be promoted through the classroom design • Provide a language-rich environment	• Plan individual instruction for content knowledge • Instructional content should include social communication skills • Be prepared to provide follow-up instruction • Focus curriculum on both language comprehension and language expression (e.g., receptive and expressive language skills) • Incorporate technology that enhances and supports fluency	• Encourage and reinforce positive behavior as it is exhibited • Provide extended "wait time" for responses from child • Allow many opportunities for the child to use language • Use concrete objects as much as possible during instruction and evaluation • Model appropriate vocalizations throughout the child's daily instruction
Hearing Impairments	• Organize seating arrangements and classroom furniture to meet the needs of all children • Seat the child near the teacher or peer buddy as necessary (this holds especially true if the child is relying on residual hearing) • When planning the environment take into consideration the external stimuli that might impact a child's use of specific technologies such as hearing aids or cochlear implants	• Plan individual instruction for content knowledge • Be prepared to provide follow-up instruction • Consider the need for interpreters when designing instructional content • Plan for instruction using more frequent visual materials • Plan group work with the individual student's needs taken into account	• Encourage and reinforce positive behavior as it is exhibited • Avoid turning your back to the child when speaking to him or her • Embed the use of graphic organizers to assist with instructional organization • Integrate sign language with children throughout the day
Vision Impairments	• Organize seating arrangements and classroom furniture to meet the needs of all children; clear pathways as necessary • Seat the child near the teacher or peer buddy as necessary • Evaluate classroom lighting (e.g., brightness and contrast) to determine its effect on the child • Evaluate the size of images and the student's needs when planning the environment	• Plan individual instruction for content knowledge • Be prepared to provide follow-up instruction • Incorporate orientation and mobility skills into curriculum • Design instruction to include auditory models and hands-on manipulatives	• Encourage and reinforce positive behavior as it is exhibited • Provide an introduction and sequence of events prior to instruction • Instruction and evaluation can be optimized through the use of optical devices or Braille access software • Locate and use books with large print during group presentations • Provide instruction considering perceptual issues • Use concrete objects and sensory materials as much as possible during instruction and evaluation

Table 2, continued

Disability	Classroom Environment	Curriculum Content	Instruction/Evaluation
Orthopedic Impairments	• Organize seating arrangements and classroom furniture to meet the needs of all children; check for accessibility • Design the environment to overcome architectural barriers • Seat the child near the teacher or peer buddy for additional assistance as needed • Evaluate the environment and make adjustments to furniture, writing utensils, coat racks, and art materials • Lower or secure furniture as necessary • Evaluate the portability of the materials within the environment	• Plan individual instruction for content knowledge • Be prepared to provide follow-up instruction • If deemed necessary, develop a healthcare plan that is individualized to meet the student's needs	• Encourage and reinforce positive behavior as it is exhibited • Provide assistive technology devices, bookstands, or switches to facilitate instruction and evaluation • Use concrete objects as much as possible during instruction and evaluation
Developmental Disabilities	• Organize seating arrangements and classroom furniture to meet the needs of all children • Seat the child near the teacher or peer buddy as necessary • Provide soft background music • Be prepared to support the child's activity or assign a peer buddy • Evaluate the environment and make adjustments to furniture, writing utensils, coat racks, and art materials	• Plan individual instruction for content knowledge • Be prepared to provide follow-up instruction • Provide consistent classroom schedule and structure that engages all students • Use concrete objects when conducting mathematics activities • Simplify complexity of expected tasks through task analysis • Offer choices for activities that are limited in number	• Encourage and reinforce positive behavior as it is exhibited • Provide more repetition and examples • Use simple instructions during lessons • Monitor instruction and ask for feedback during lessons • Show a sample of the work that is expected from the child • Provide extended "wait time" for responses from the child • Provide time for the child to complete his or her work • Use concrete objects as much as possible during instruction and evaluation

SUCCESSFUL INCLUSION STRATEGIES FOR EARLY CHILDHOOD TEACHERS

Disability	Classroom Environment	Curriculum Content	Instruction/Evaluation
Traumatic Brain Injury (TBI)	◆ Organize seating arrangements and classroom furniture to meet the needs of all children (the environment should encourage mobility) ◆ Seat the child near the teacher or peer buddy as necessary ◆ Provide soft background music	◆ Plan individual instruction for content knowledge, taking into account that the learning and curriculum needs of students with TBI are continuously changing ◆ Be prepared to provide follow-up instruction ◆ If deemed necessary, develop a healthcare plan that is individualized to meet the student's needs	◆ Encourage and reinforce positive behavior as it is exhibited ◆ Use concrete objects as much as possible during instruction and evaluation

technology and the structure of the physical environment creates a greater opportunity for the child's success.

Young children with moderate/severe disabilities and multiple disabilities must be afforded the same opportunities as their typically developing peers in activities and instruction. Eight specific ways are provided to teachers to help them in modifying curriculum for young children with moderate/severe and multiple disabilities (Horn, Chambers, & Saito, as cited in Raver, 2009):

1. *Environmental support*: Environmental support involves changing or altering the environment (physical, social, and temporal) to increase participation and learning. For example, you may move furniture around to accommodate wheelchair access to specific areas of the room.

2. *Material adaptations*: Material adaptations include modifying specific materials to increase the likelihood that a child can become more independent when he or she participates in an activity. For example, if a child has a weak grasp, you may need to use Velcro® straps to adhere paintbrushes, crayons, or pencils to his or her hand. More information on material adaptations is found in Chapter 11.

3. *Special equipment*: Often special commercial or teacher-made materials are necessary to assist a child in participating in an activity. This equipment may include high- or low-tech assistive technology devices. An example of special equipment is the use of a supportive chair or a communication device built into a computer.

4. *Use of children's preferences*: Many children respond well to high preference reinforcers such as singing songs, tickling, and stickers. These types of materials or activities should be integrated into activities to increase motivation. Selecting preferences should be done on an individual basis.

5. *Simplification of the activity*: Many times a specific activity can be performed by the child with special needs if the activity is simplified or the number of steps involved in the activity are reduced. A task analysis (additional information on task analysis is found on p. 152) can be performed to determine how many steps are involved in an activity. For example, a child may be able to complete a puzzle if three of the five pieces are already connected.

6. *Adult support*: Adults can provide support to children with special needs in multiple ways such as providing praise and encouragement, providing hand-over-hand assistance, and modeling appropriate play behaviors.

7. *Peer support*: Peers can serve as supports to children with special needs in many of the same ways as adults do. This can only occur if peers are given proper training and supervision. Peer support should never replace teacher assistance and supervision.

8. *Invisible support*: Invisible support is simply rearranging naturally occurring activities so that a child can participate more fully in them. This is done without the knowledge of the children. For example, if a class project involves all children placing an object on a piece of butcher paper, the butcher paper is placed at a lower than usual level so that a child in a wheelchair would be able to access this without the support of being lifted to a higher level or without the paper being lowered for him when it was his turn to adhere the object.

Although each chapter in this book provides general recommendations based on the specific disability addressed, Figure 1 (Weinfeld & Davis, 2008) provides some best practices for providing appropriate adaptations and accommodations.

PREPARING FOR A SUCCESSFUL INCLUSION PROGRAM

The success of an inclusion program is heavily weighted on the actions and attitudes of the teachers in the classroom. Cook and colleagues (2008) identified 15 strategies that will help prepare the way to successfully include children with special needs in the preschool program:

1. Meet with the child's parents prior to implementing the inclusion model to gather more information from the parent regarding the child's special interests, specific problems, and solutions.

2. Children should be phased into the program slowly and only after the previously noted parent visit.

3. Take time to prepare the children already enrolled in the center so they can ask questions and you can assist them in understanding their fears.

Research has revealed that the principles put forth here are the best practices for providing appropriate adaptations and accommodations for kids with learning difficulties in order to ensure access to appropriate educational opportunities.

❏ Accommodations used in assessments should parallel accommodations that are integrated into classroom instruction.

❏ The adaptations/accommodations are aligned with the educational impact of the individual student's disability and the adaptations/accommodations are aligned with the needs described in the student's IEP or 504 Plan.

❏ The adaptations/accommodations are based upon the strengths of the student.

❏ Accommodations are based on what students need in order to be provided with an equal opportunity to show what they know without impediment of their disability.

❏ Assessments allow students, while using appropriate accommodations, to demonstrate their skills without interference from their disabilities.

❏ After selecting and providing appropriate adaptations/accommodations, their impact on the performance of the individual student is evaluated and only those that are effective are continued.

❏ The adaptations/accommodations are reviewed, revised, and when appropriate, faded over time, allowing the student to move from dependence to independence.

❏ A multidisciplinary team, which considers the input of the parent and student, decides upon the adaptations/accommodations.

❏ The appropriate adaptations/accommodations and the rationale for each of them are shared with all staff members who work with the student.

FIGURE 1. Adaptations and accommodations checklist.

Note. From *Special Needs Advocacy Resource Book* (p. 39) by R. Weinfeld and M. Davis, 2008, Waco, TX: Prufrock Press. Copyright © 2008, Prufrock Press. Reprinted with permission.

4. Answer children's questions honestly. Although it is not necessary to use lengthy responses, it is important to be honest in your answers.
5. Address the fears and concerns of the families and parents of children with and without special needs.
6. Encourage and support all parents.
7. Remain positive.
8. Be realistic.
9. Create simple rules and guidelines for expected classroom behavior.

10. Find opportunities to highlight the specific strengths that the child with special needs has.

11. Create opportunities for the child with special needs to serve as a helper in the classroom. This will prevent the child with special needs from always being the student who needs help.

12. Use creative strategies to adapt and change the environment to meet the needs of the children in the class rather than trying to change the child.

13. Provide training to staff that focuses on facilitating peer interactions.

14. Provide a structured environment.

15. Do not expect too much of yourself or the situation. (p. 162).

Following the aforementioned guidelines will assist you in meeting the needs of all of the students in your classroom. Open lines of communication and collaboration between all those involved with the child with special needs will strengthen the probability that the specific goals and objectives designed for the child will be mastered within the inclusive setting.

CHAPTER 3

Sam

A CHILD WITH AUTISM SPECTRUM DISORDER

Sam's teacher thought to herself after the morning's Circle Time, "Sam's having a good day today. I hope the rest of the day moves as smoothly for us." Sam made it through most of the early daily routine with limited disruption to the flow of class activities. His focus on the lesson, though somewhat dreamy, appeared to be as attentive as the other children's, and he answered one of the questions that she asked. Although he looked at the materials shown to the group, a close observation indicated that his mind was elsewhere. Most of the time, he rocked slowly back and forth in his place, but his actions did not seem to disturb the other children in the group.

During Center Time, Sam approached his selected tasks with a quiet determination, but a joyous attitude did not emerge in his play as it does with most preschoolers. On occasion, he appeared only to be going through the motions of putting puzzles together, and later, participating in block play with his peers. Even when his teacher talked to him, his responses were minimal, and his dialogue with other children seemed incoherent.

Then, a crisis emerged. A visitor to the classroom disrupted the rest of Sam's day. When Mrs. Moore, the school's secretary and someone Sam recognized from previous visits, left the room after a brief discussion with Sam's teacher, Sam wanted to go with her. Emitting a loud yelp, he ran to the classroom door as Mrs. Moore was closing it behind her, screaming over and over, "Sam go with you! Sam go with you!" Mrs. Moore pried Sam's hands from the doorknob while saying as calmly as possible, "You need to stay here, Sam. I have to go back to work." His teacher was on her knees beside him saying, "Sam, you need to stay here with us. This is your classroom, and you need to stay here."

OVERVIEW OF AUTISM SPECTRUM DISORDER

Autism is a developmental disorder that results in the delay in the normal patterns of development. However, the actual diagnosis of autism often is misunderstood because of the wide range and variation in the severity of its impact on development. Lynch (2009) provided the following definition:

> There is considerable variation in the severity of autism and its impact on development, and it is considered a spectrum of disorders, or autism spectrum disorder (ASD). The term *spectrum* is used because children with autism differ widely from one another. Some children with autism may be able to read and perform academic skills close to grade level, while others will have considerably more severe cognitive problems. Some children with autism are fluent speakers, while others may be nonverbal. (p. 5)

Throughout this chapter we will use the term *autism* to refer to children on the autism spectrum.

Early diagnosis of autism is essential, as the earlier the intervention begins, the more effective the treatment results. Often, parents and early caregivers are the first to notice specific characteristics of autism in young children. For example, preschool children diagnosed with autism often have limited interactions with peers, do not respond to their names, and show little interest interacting with others. The text revision of the fourth edition of the *Diagnostic and Statistical Manual of Mental Disorders* (DSM-IV-TR; American Psychiatric Association [APA], 2000), a reference tool used by psychologists, psychiatrists, and physicians for information regarding diagnoses and treatment options for numerous disorders, established the diagnostic criteria for autism. Four diagnostic categories are addressed. Lynch (2009) defined these categories below along with what a classroom teacher might see in relation to each category.

1. *Qualitative impairment in social interaction*: A teacher may see a child who does not look at peers or smile at them, a child who does not play with other children, or a child who does not initiate contact with others. In addition, a teacher may see a child who does not play with other children and tends to play alone.
2. *Qualitative impairment in communication*: A teacher may see a child who does not participate in pretend or creative play unless taught to do so, a child who answers questions in short responses (often single-word responses), a child who does speak but may lack the ability to initiate and continue conversations, or a child with limited to no speech.
3. *Restricted and repetitive patterns of interest and behavior*: A teacher may see a child interested in only a few topics within the classroom (e.g., dinosaurs, Disney characters), a child carrying around odd objects, a child using repetitive actions (e.g., flapping, spinning, jumping, hand flicking), or a child who is preoccupied with parts of objects.
4. *Delay or deviation in development*: A delay or deviation from typical development in the areas of communication, socialization, and imaginative play needs to be noted before age 3 for autism to be diagnosed.

In addition to the inclusion of categories for diagnosis, the *DSM-IV-TR* also classified different forms of autism. As previously mentioned, the term *spectrum* is used because many children with autism fall somewhere on a continuum ranging from severe to mild. There are five types of autism spectrum disorders: autism, Pervasive Developmental Disorder-Not Otherwise Specified (PDD-NOS), Asperger's syndrome, childhood disintegrative disorder, and Rett's syndrome. Each of the forms differ in the diagnostic criteria and the specific implications that the characteristics of the disability will have on classroom instruction. Some key differences in the diagnostic criteria of each are as follows:

- *PDD-NOS*: Onset of the characteristics occur after age 3, or when not all criteria for autism is met, yet the child shows a severe and pervasive impairment in development of reciprocal social interaction or verbal and nonverbal communication skills.
- *Asperger's syndrome*: Most children with Asperger's syndrome have average to above-average intelligence and have met the

DSM-IV-TR criteria for "qualitative impairment in social interaction, and present a substantial problem with social, occupational or other areas of functioning. However, there is no communication or cognitive delay in development" (Lynch, 2009, p. 8). As Willis (2006) noted:

> These children have been described as having difficulty with coordination, vocal tone (they tend to speak in a monotone), depression, violent reactions to change, and they have a tendency for ritualistic behaviors. In addition, children with Asperger's syndrome may develop an intense obsession with objects or activities. (p. 19)

- *Childhood disintegrative disorder*: Children with childhood disintegrative disorder develop normally throughout the first 2 years of life. However, these children will begin to show signs of autistic behavior shortly thereafter. During the ages of 3–4, language, social, cognitive, and motor skills often are lost. Children will seem to forget how to do things including toilet training and play skills.
- *Rett's syndrome*: Children with Rett's syndrome develop normally and then around 18 months start to display characteristic hand movements such as wringing, tapping, and putting their hands in their mouths. They also will continue to lose skills throughout their life. This particular disorder is predominantly seen in girls and is caused by a genetic mutation.

The eligibility criteria listed above is a standard reference point for teachers and family members. However, a child is not diagnosed with autism without a comprehensive assessment, which usually consists of a review of the family history and the child's developmental progress, and a physical exam by a medical doctor. Knowing the family history is important, because research has linked a genetic component to autism. If a child is receiving an autism assessment, part of the assessment may involve an observation by a psychologist in the child's natural setting, which would include his classroom. The psychologist might examine characteristics of the child, such as his ability to socialize and play, his ability to make eye contact, and how he responds to his surroundings. Often, during the comprehensive assessment, psychologists may identify additional special needs that coexist with autism. Some examples of coexisting conditions include seizures, cognitive delays, sensory issues, and speech and language disorders. Coexisting special needs may or may not have a direct link to autism. For example, it would be inaccurate to say that autism causes seizures or that seizures cause autism. This simply would not be consistent with all children with autism. However, both autism and seizures have a neurological basis, which may contribute to the high incidence of seizure activity in children with autism.

Because autism is a condition that falls within a wide spectrum of abilities, the identification of a child with autism offers little guidance to a caregiver unless the diagnosis provides information regarding the child's cognitive and social levels. Each child identified with autism will demonstrate a variety of characteristics, and interventions should be tailored to the child's specific needs. Some children with autism have limited speech and or language skills, while others do not have this difficulty.

The causes of autism remain unknown or unclear and are the subject of an increasing amount of debate. Some suggested factors that may contribute to autism include neurological problems (brain disorders), chromosomal abnormality (genetics), metabolic disorders, immune deficiency (compromised immune system), perinatal anoxia (inadequate oxygen supply to the brain at the time of birth), childhood vaccinations (resulting from Thimerosal, a mercury-based preservative found in vaccines), pesticides, oral antibiotics, and increased levels of mercury in the environment. These are only suggested factors, and there is much debate regarding the validity of some of these factors. Although no cure for autism has been identified, experts agree that children diagnosed with autism need early intervention services. There are many treatment options available for children with autism.

As with all children, one treatment does not fit all. A team of experts including, but not limited to, educators, related service personnel, therapists, and the family should determine the appropriate treatment for a child with autism. A great deal of debate revolves around the most effective treatment for children with autism. Some psychiatrists recommend the use of medication to treat autism, while others recommend a change in a child's nutritional intake. A sampling of this type of intervention involves a variety of measures such as identification of food allergies, detoxification of metals within the body, and special diets (casein free/

gluten free). Most authorities agree that early intense intervention based on Applied Behavior Analysis has the strongest research base for treatment success.

WHAT TEACHERS NEED TO KNOW ABOUT AUTISM SPECTRUM DISORDER

The diagnosis of autism rarely occurs prior to 18 months. Therefore, many caregivers in childcare facilities may be among the first to suspect that specific behaviors a child has are different from those of children who are typically developing. Some general characteristics of autism that a teacher or caregiver might report to a family member are:

- lack of interest in other peers,
- inability to understand and use language,
- inability to participate in shared conversations,
- inability to engage in social interactions,
- inability to participate in pretend play activities (e.g., using a pretend plate or cup),
- inability to point to or request specific objects,
- lack of eye contact with others,
- unusual fixation with specific objects,
- lack of interest in touching or playing with toys, and
- failure to point to items of interest in the environment by the age of 18 months.

The characteristics above are indicators that a concern may exist, but evaluators should not use them as a sole factor in determining that a child has autism. A complete and thorough evaluation is necessary to make this determination. Often, an initial screening is done prior to a full evaluation. In this case, the parent may be interviewed and the child may be observed performing specific tasks. In a situation where a child has not been diagnosed with autism, but is undergoing assessment, you, as caregiver, may need to fill out a questionnaire such as the Modified Checklist for Autism in Toddlers (M-CHAT). The M-CHAT is a screening tool used for early identification of autism in young children. The answers to the questionnaire assist in the accurate diagnosis of autism in young children and toddlers. A copy of the M-CHAT, along with specific information regarding its scoring and use, is available at http://www.dbpeds.org/media/mchat.pdf. It is important to note that the M-CHAT is intended to be used as a screening tool. If results indicate a possibility that a child shows characteristics of autism, then that child should receive a full evaluation, conducted by a professional trained in the area of autism. Other screening tools used to gather diagnostic data are the Autism Screening Instrument for Educational Planning-3, and the Gilliam Autism Rating Scale-2.

Once specialists identify that a child has autism, the school or center, family, therapists, and physicians will need to work together to ensure the successful implementation of an intervention plan. The purpose of the assessment is to not only determine and diagnose the problem, but also to develop interventions and determine program effectiveness. The development of the child's IEP will weigh heavily on family and teacher input as well as the results outlined in the assessment report. It is very important that

> when reading a report on a child with autism, one should remember that how the child scores will depend on a number of factors: the child's interest in the task, the effort the child gave, the rapport with the examiner, the attention and language requirements of the task, and whether the child understood what was expected. Also, the testing process usually interrupts the child's routine and removes the child from the familiar environment. Both of these conditions are difficult for children with autism. However, teachers can gain valuable understanding when they read reports with a focus on what the child is able to do and where the child will need assistance. (Lynch, 2009, p. 15)

Depending on the type of intervention that the child receives, and his or her IEP/IFSP objectives, your role as the caregiver or teacher may change. Some children with autism have a treatment plan that involves sensory stimulation or integration. If a child in the classroom needs this type of intervention, your role might involve providing various techniques to facilitate the child's sensory responses throughout the day (rubbing, touching, movement, and balancing activities). This chapter provides specific information and strategies for working with children with autism in the section called "Autism Spectrum Disorder: Inclusive

Classroom Strategies" on pp. 43–58. If an approach to serving children with autism includes the use of Applied Behavior Analysis, you might expect to see a consultant, Board Certified Behavior Analyst, or behavioral specialist coming to the facility to provide one-on-one instruction with the child. This type of intervention often is used with young children identified with autism. Each child with autism has varying individual needs. These needs are noted in the child's IEP/IFSP and determine the specific professionals who work with the child.

Another specialist that you may need to collaborate with is a speech-language pathologist, a professional who diagnoses and treats speech and language development problems. As previously mentioned, assessment, intervention, and evaluation are successfully implemented when team members form collaborative relationships. The speech-language pathologist will assess the communication development of a student with autism. In addition, a speech-language pathologist might teach a child with autism sign language, or how to utilize a Picture Exchange Communication System (PECS). PECS is a method that is employed to teach children to communicate by exchanging pictures for objects and actions. PECS includes an exchange of pictures that are removed from a book or binder. This system mimics natural conversation as the exchange of the picture replicates the exchange of verbal communication. This system differs from other picture communication systems because the child is not taught to only point to a specific picture that reflects the request or action but to actually exchange the pictures with another person similar to the vocal exchanges made when having a conversation.

The speech-language pathologist may want to introduce you to simple signs to integrate into your classroom instruction or may ask you to help reinforce specific skills through various activities. Typically, the first signs that a teacher should use in her classroom are those high-frequency words used throughout the day. For example, if "line up" is said numerous times throughout the day, this would be a key word or phrase to pair with sign language.

Services that are provided to a student with autism by a speech-language therapist may be direct or indirect. The type of service will depend on the specific needs of the child. A direct service provider would involve the speech-language therapist providing services to the child. An indirect model often is provided when a speech-language therapist trains other individuals to provide speech services to the child.

The type of services that the child receives should be documented in the IEP or IFSP.

Occupational and physical therapists often are involved in the child's intervention plan. An occupational therapist (OT) works primarily with assisting the child with sensory issues and fine motor deficits. In addition, the OT works on self-help skills such as toileting and self-feeding. A physical therapist (PT) focuses on large motor issues. Collaboration is essential in a child's progress. The occupational therapist defines ways for you to improve the child's ability to interpret sensory input and utilize his fine motor skills. The physical therapist provides information about improving the child's large motor development. Many children with autism may be receiving sensory integration therapy (SI). SI therapy involves the OT and/or PT working with the child to improve his or her ability to process sensory information in the brain. "The results of research studies to establish the effectiveness of SI therapy are controversial" (Winter, 2007, p. 131). Many parents have indicated success with having their child receive SI therapy. The therapist implementing this service may request that the classroom teacher follow through with some of the interventions throughout the day.

AUTISM SPECTRUM DISORDER: INCLUSIVE CLASSROOM STRATEGIES

Family Interventions

Families whose children have a diagnosis of autism spectrum disorder (ASD) need long-term support as they deal with specific characteristics associated with ASD that range from mild to severe. Children with autism continue to demonstrate characteristics as adults and, although some are capable of achieving independence in adulthood, many need supervision throughout their lives. Families need assistance in determining how to help their child interact with others, participate in pretend play, and develop friendships with peers outside the family group. Children with autism benefit from a team approach among families, professionals, and classroom teachers or caregivers.

Classroom Interventions

Teachers need training to develop positive, age-appropriate behaviors within children diagnosed with autism spectrum disorder. Classroom instruction is critical in helping children diagnosed with autism with:

- conflict resolution,
- how to make friends,
- learning others' perspectives, and
- encouraging trustworthiness and loyalty to others (Turnbull, Turnbull, & Wehmeyer, 2007).

It is essential to recognize that the child with autism needs information about social play, as well as information about how to play with toys and how to get along with peers. Modeling these behaviors and helping children with autism observe others who have the necessary skills is part of the curriculum in an inclusive classroom. Modeling involves having the child watch the adult demonstrate the task, and then having the child perform the same task that was demonstrated. This process is a very powerful strategy used when teaching young children with special needs.

EFFECTIVE CLASSROOM ENVIRONMENT

Creating an effective classroom environment for a child with autism will involve some preparation on your part. Children with autism often require a structured physical environment. To create such an environment, try reducing clutter and visual distractions, reducing auditory distractions (e.g., lessen excess noise levels by laying out area rugs or putting up wall hangings that absorb noise), and limiting the amount of open space in the classroom. Clearly defined areas will add more structure to the classroom setting. Not only are the classroom arrangement and environment important factors to consider; you also should examine the daily routine. Children with autism respond better to a consistent, predictable, and well-structured routine.

PROMOTING ATTENDING SKILLS

Children with autism need to learn how to focus on environmental factors that affect learning. Competing stimuli often distract children with autism, so they must learn to prioritize what is important in the educational setting. This requires assistance from trained teachers. All children must learn to pay attention to visual and vocal cues, but you may need to use individualized instructional strategies and various sensory techniques (e.g., touching objects or looking at them closely) to help the child with autism pay attention during lessons.

HAVING ROUTINE SCHEDULES AND ACTIVITIES

Predictable environments are critical for children with autism. The organizational structure of the classroom (furniture, classroom centers, bulletin boards, instructional materials, schedules, and so on) will either assist or hinder children with autism in their abilities to learn. They need clear physical and visual boundaries and consistent daily schedules that are easy to understand and follow. Daily schedules are more appropriate if they are paired with pictures to represent each part of the day (see Figure 2). Classroom posters that show center choices along with center labels, timetables for the day, how to perform self-help skills (such as brushing their teeth or hanging their jackets), and clearly defined classroom areas are important to the functioning of children with autism.

USING SONGS TO FACILITATE SMOOTH TRANSITIONS

Traditionally, teachers use musical cues to help children understand the order of activities or events that children will participate in throughout the day. The songs serve as a cue to what will be occurring next on the child's schedule. For example, if it is time to stop participating in Center Time and move to tables for Snack Time, teachers sing a song familiar to the children as a cue to begin cleaning up their respective centers. Often, these songs are merely chants, but some teachers make up words for familiar tunes to use for Transition Time. Preparing children for another part of the daily schedule avoids chaos and allows them to change activities with a minimum of fuss. A multitude of books are available at local teacher supply stores that contain songs and other transition activities.

OFFERING CHOICE MAKING

Learning how to make choices in the classroom is an important foundation for children, as they will need this skill when making decisions throughout childhood and adulthood. Generally, teachers introduce centers to their students at the beginning of the school year (usually only a few centers at a time to protect children from being overwhelmed). Once children know their choices, a classroom poster or bulletin board

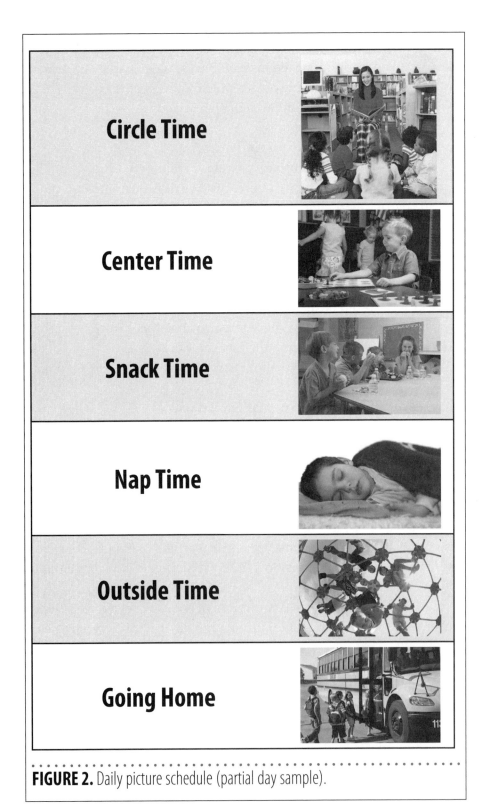

FIGURE 2. Daily picture schedule (partial day sample).

will define which ones are available. Many teachers allow children to change their choice during the time allotted for center play, with nametags available to them so they can make a new selection. Other teachers tell their children that they must stick with their original decision and remain in the center they have chosen. With either procedure, children learn how to make decisions, and they develop emotional competence with their choice making.

TEACHING MEMORY STRATEGIES

Children with autism have a range of learning abilities, and many with Asperger's syndrome are highly skilled in memory tasks (Turnbull et al., 2007). For young children who need help improving their memory, songs, rhymes, and special chants can help them recall information they need in the classroom. Most preschool teachers use these strategies naturally as they teach the ABCs ("The Alphabet Song") and numbers (e.g., using nursery rhymes such as "One, Two, Buckle My Shoe"). Using memory techniques during one-on-one time with children with autism helps them to relate to the content presented in lessons.

PROMOTING RELATIONSHIPS WITH PEERS

One priority should be to help children with social development. Children with autism tend to be isolated, yet they can learn from their typically developing peers if you take time to discuss appropriate behaviors that others demonstrate. For example, you might say to a child, "Did you notice how Madison asked if she could join the children who are in the Home Living Center? You could ask the same question. Which center do you want to go to? I'll help you join the play." Individualized instruction is the key element in promoting positive relationships in the classroom.

USING SOCIAL SCRIPTS/SOCIAL STORIES

Another strategy that you and families can use with children of all ages is the social script. Social scripts present a social situation that children can use to identify appropriate responses that they may recall at a later time to help them monitor their own behavior. Examples might include developing a story about building a block structure with a group of other children, what to do if conflicts arise about sharing toys, or how to prepare the table for classroom snacks. You might write stories that involve school situations, and the children's families might write stories about other aspects of the child's life. These stories present opportunities for children to understand others' viewpoints and learn how to behave in a variety of social situations (Lynch & Simpson, 2007). Consequently, children with autism are able to make judgments about social activities that allow them to control their own responses to social situations they encounter in daily life.

Carol Gray (1991) identified specific sentence formats that can be used in developing social stories. Social stories are designed to teach a social routine such as "greeting your friends" or "taking turns during block play." "Social stories follow an elicit format of approximately 5–10 sentences describing the social skill, the appropriate behavior, and others viewpoints of the actions" (Spencer, Simpson, & Lynch, 2008, p. 59). The use of a social story proves beneficial to students with ASD as the stories can be easily assimilated in the general education setting where reading and literacy activities are being conducted. In addition, the social story or social script should not be used in isolation. The story should first be created (allow the child to participate in the development of the story) and introduced. After the child is familiar with the steps presented in the social story, the information then can become part of the child's daily intervention. For example, if a story is created that addresses greeting peers outside of the classroom, visual cues can be used while walking to the bus, to recess, or departing from school. You would not pull the story out during the walk in the hall, but a cue such as a raised hand to the chest may signal a reminder to the child to follow the steps that previously were presented in the social story and modeled in the classroom. The following is a sample social story that depicts the appropriate sentence design for the story (Spencer et al., 2008):

Recess Time

We like to play with toys during recess time. (descriptive sentence)

When it is time to clean up after recess time, my teacher sings the clean up song. (descriptive sentence)

Sometimes we are having fun playing and do not want to clean up. (descriptive sentence)

After we clean up our toys we can go inside for snacks. (descriptive sentence)

Even when we want to keep playing, we pick up our toys. (directive sentence)

My teacher is happy when we pick up our toys. (perspective sentence)

It is important to keep our toys neat and to pick up. (perspective sentence)

I will remember to pick up my toys when I hear the clean up song at recess. (control sentence; p. 60)

Additional strategies are employed to teach social interaction to children with autism including Music Therapy, Circle of Friends, Comic Strip Conversations, and Cooperative Learning Groups. The Web toolbox in Figure 3 provides an overview of popular social skills programs along with a respective Web site to obtain additional information on each program.

Behavioral Momentum

Behavioral momentum is an intervention strategy that requires teachers to collect data about children who have challenging behaviors. Once the data are studied, teachers can formulate a plan of action to assist children in learning classroom rules and routines. Children are praised when they comply with expected behaviors. Eventually, when children demonstrate compliant behaviors, praise becomes unnecessary.

Behavior Analysis

Many families of children with autism have become familiar with the field of Applied Behavior Analysis (ABA). ABA techniques are based on the basic principle that behavior can be changed by changing the child's environment, specifically the events that occur before and after the target behavior. Board Certified Behavior Analysts (BCBA) have successfully demonstrated their skills and competence in using techniques of behavior change. Typically, ABA is a very intense program (with some children receiving as much as 40 hours per week) where tasks are analyzed and rewards are utilized to increase skill acquisition. If a specific behavior is reinforced it is likely that the behavior will be repeated. This type of service is individualized and the program developed is frequently evaluated to determine the student's progress toward specific goals, and to set new observable, measurable goals. As a teacher, you should be aware that a BCBA might be involved in a child's intervention plan.

Title	URL Address	Description
Interactive Collaborative Autism Network	http://www.autismnetwork.org	This site is targeted to reach teachers, parents, and youth with autism and is maintained by the ICAN project. The site covers a wide array of topics (called *modules*) on characteristics, assessments, and interventions (academic, behavioral, communication, environment, sensory, and social). These modules are comprehensive and informative with accurate and interesting information. The social module is well developed and gives very detailed information on specific interventions that teachers and parents can implement.
Cooperative Learning Network	http://www.lcandler.web.aplus.net	Cooperative Learning Network is a Web site maintained by a teacher, Laura Candler, and does a good job highlighting the steps in teaching cooperative learning.
About.com: Special Education	http://specialed.about.com/lr/supporting_weak_social_skills_in_the_classroom/2912/2	This is a good site that lists articles written about supporting social skills in the classroom. There is a wide variety of articles providing a plethora of information about improving social skills for children that need it.
Polyxo.com: Teaching Children With Autism	http://www.polyxo.com/socialstories	This Web site has a wealth of practical and accurate information for teachers of children with autism. It provides a good deal of social stories and information on how to introduce them and use them in the classroom.
Lovaas Institute Blog	http://www.lovaas.com/blog/archives/15-Teaching-Social-Skills-to-Children-with-Autism.html	This Web site describes the steps in teaching social skills based on the Lovaas method. In addition, this site also gives a link to free research articles on the subject.
Teaching Social Skills to Kids Who Don't Have Them	http://maxweber.hunter.cuny.edu/pub/eres/EDSPC715_MCINTYRE/SocialSkills.html	This is an extremely helpful site for teachers wanting to teach social skills and offers a way to evaluate social skills curriculum.
NLD on the Web	http://www.nldontheweb.org	This site has links to research articles about working with children with nonverbal learning disabilities (NLD). It is not specific for autism but children with NLD have some similar deficits in social skills as do children with ASD.
Inclusive Solutions	http://www.inclusive-solutions.com	This site promotes the consulting and workshop endeavors of a private group of educational psychologists promoting their consulting and workshop services. In addition to being a for-profit Web site, there is a wealth of free accessible information to support inclusion, specifically social inclusion. In addition to useful links, this site also contains information on current research and literature supporting social inclusion, free ideas and strategies, details about person-centered planning, Circle of Friends information, and an online store for books, videos, inclusion packs, training equipment, toys, and T-shirts.
The West Virginia Autism Training Center: Model Preschool	http://www.marshall.edu/coe/ATC/about.htm	This Web site features a description of a Model Circle of Friends Preschool Program for young children with autism and their typically developing peers. The program incorporates best practices taken from the field of early childhood and autism.

FIGURE 3. When students need help with social skills: A Web toolbox.

Note. Adapted from "Socialization and Children With Autism Spectrum Disorders" (p. 85) by K. Wilhite, M. C. Tripp, L. L. S. Canter, and K. Floyd, 2009, in V. G. Spencer and C. G. Simpson (Eds.), *Teaching Children With Autism in the General Classroom*, Waco, TX: Prufrock Press. Copyright © 2009, Prufrock Press. Reprinted with permission.

Figure 3, continued

Title	URL Address	Description
Social Stories	http://thegraycenter.org	Developed by Carol Gray, Social Stories and Comic Strip Conversations are used with children and adults with ASD. This center works to improve social understanding by helping individuals with ASD to communicate and interact more successfully with the people with whom they live and work.
The National Autistic Society	http://www.nas.org.uk	This Web site provides an autism helpline. This society is based in London. It provides information about the definition and characteristics of autism and Asperger's syndrome. You can retrieve current information about interventions and behavior management skills. Additionally, there is information for parents about diet and other strategies.
Baltimore County Public Schools	http://www.bcps.org/offices/ special_ed/altmsa_autism/ Music-Therapy-Page.html	This is just one Web site of many that discusses specialized services for children within the autism spectrum. Music therapy services are provided in this school district to assist students to be functional participants in their educational environment. Music therapists provide direct and consulting services to a student when assessed to show that music therapy is needed to assist in gaining IEP progress.

Applying the Strategies

As Mrs. Moore, the school's secretary and someone Sam recognized from previous visits, left the room after a brief discussion with Sam's teacher, Sam wanted to go with her. Emitting a loud yelp, he ran to the classroom door as she was closing it behind her, screaming over and over, "Sam go with you! Sam go with you!" Mrs. Moore pried Sam's hands from the doorknob while she said as calmly as possible, "You need to stay here, Sam. I have to go back to work." Sam's teacher was on her knees beside him saying, "Sam, you need to stay here with us. This is your classroom, and you need to stay here."

This particular episode was not unusual for Sam, and Randi, his teacher, had learned early in the school year how to handle his outbursts. When Sam began the school year, she had taken time to make sure that he understood the basic classroom rules. For several weeks, she spent a few minutes of her day (usually as soon as Sam arrived in the morning) demonstrating the appropriate behavioral responses she expected of him and the other children. Although his outbursts continued through-out the year, they become less frequent as he adjusted to the consistent classroom schedule and learned how to interact with others around him. The following are some other specific strategies Sam's teacher used.

Working With the Whole Class

Sam's teacher incorporated the following strategies for behaviors and techniques that would affect her entire class.

- *Post the daily schedule*: Sam's teacher wrote the daily schedule on a classroom poster, including photographs to help him understand what Center Time, Circle Time, Outdoor Play, lunch, and other daily events were and the order in which they occurred. Often, in her early morning discussions with Sam, she used the poster to help him remember what the day would be like at school. Other students could see the poster to help them stay on track as well.

- *Model and encourage the use of classroom centers*: Teachers generally take time at the beginning of each school year to show children how to use the centers in their classrooms. Children with autism need special instruction and demonstration to ensure success in each center. For example, Sam's teacher encouraged Sam to use the Listening Center several times during the week. At first, she modeled the behavior he needed to use while listening to CDs and looking at books, and with experience, he became quite skilled at performing this activity independently.

- *Use sequence cards to assist in daily activities*: Providing sequence cards that demonstrate the specific steps or actions to be taken will help a child with ASD understand the expectations the teacher has of him. Cards can be actual photos or line drawings illustrating a set of events or actions such as hanging up a coat on a coat rack.

- *Communicate with families*: Sam's teacher sent regular communications to the families of children enrolled in her class. She communicated more frequently with Sam's family, reporting successes or any outbursts Sam had. She maintained a positive attitude about his behavior. Sam's teacher also interviewed Sam's parents to determine the things at school that Sam really enjoyed doing. She then utilized this information to create reinforcers for Sam when he achieved specific goals that were set for him.

Working With Individual Children

When working one-on-one with Sam, his teacher incorporated the following strategies:

- *Use gestures and questions*: When children gathered for Circle Time each day, Sam's teacher would look at him and point to her own eyes to remind him that he needed to look at her while she was talking and developing the lesson. Occasionally, she would ask him a question to help him focus on the presentation. If he demonstrated good attention, she made a comment to him about his behavior as Circle Time ended. For example, she might say, "I could tell you were listening well today." She also paired her comments with appropriate facial expressions (like smiles) and gestures.

- *Help with Center Time choices*: Before Center Time each day, Sam's teacher took the time to help him make a choice that would be appropriate for him. She often helped him talk to the other children in the center about joining them and modeled how to play with the materials in the center.

- *Facilitate social interactions*: Sam's teacher observed Sam's play during Center Time, and she designed opportunities that helped improve his relationships with his peers. Sam's activities involved sharing, cooperation, and taking turns. When she saw difficulties on Sam's part, she would step in and talk him through the steps he needed to take to maintain positive behaviors. Some of the children began helping Sam learn to share toys and take turns using verbal comments they had learned in the small-group discussions.

- *Create visual boundaries*: When Sam put puzzles together, his teacher put the frame and puzzle pieces on a carpet square. This helped him visually attend to the puzzle he was working on instead of picking up pieces that belonged to other children's puzzles. When he was playing with playdough, she placed it on a cookie sheet so that Sam would have a visual boundary while he played.

- *Read books about making friends*: Sam's teacher shared a number of books that addressed the issue of making friends. Examples include *Friends at School* by Rochelle Bennett (1995), *Making Friends* by Fred Rogers (1996), and *Will I Have a Friend?* by Miriam Cohen (2009). Sam particularly enjoyed Fred Rogers' title, and he often asked his teacher to read it. Sam's teacher encouraged his family to purchase the book so they could read it to him at home.

- *Use behavioral momentum.* Behavioral momentum interventions are designed to build a student's "momentum" for being able to complete assigned tasks or activities. Consider a ball that is rolling—once it gets going down a hill (gains momentum), it continues to roll. This is similar to behavior—once the desired behavior occurs (the more we engage in it), it is likely that the behavior will continue to occur. In general, this strategy attempts to create a momentum of compliance. If the teacher is able to get Sam to start to follow specific instructions, then the premise is that he will continue to follow subsequent instructions (even those he dislikes). An example that Sam's teacher, Randi, encountered was clean-up time. Sam often had difficulty responding to his teacher's request to put the toys away. His teacher began to collect data to determine when he appropriately responded to her requests. She recorded the instructions that Sam responded to throughout the day. She was able to create a list of four instructions that Sam followed. She started to give very clear, short directions to Sam at clean-up time (she gave these quietly to not draw attention to Sam). The instructions were given in a way that was positive and not controlling. For instance, she would say, "Pick up the car from the floor." If he did this, she would offer immediate verbal praise and move to the next instruction. "Place the car on the shelf" was her next instruction for Sam. This process was continued with praise being offered after each instruction was followed. The sequential steps lead to the completion of clean up. When Sam was at the point where he had to return to his seat, the momentum of complying to the smaller steps lead him to respond the final step. When Sam followed Randi's instructions, she praised him for following instructions. Once Sam had learned how to respond to Randi's requests, she was able to reduce the clean-up steps to simply "Clean up and return to your seat."

- *Hold hands during transitions:* When children left the classroom for Outdoor Play, moved to the school's library, or departed at the end of the school day, Sam's teacher always took Sam's hand as the group walked to their destination. This strategy helped Sam stay with the group and not be distracted or even overwhelmed by other activities going on in the school. Some children are more willing to take your hand if you hold it out to them as opposed to grasping their hand. Randi gradually faded hand holding as Sam learned to remain with the group while transitioning.

- *Provide individualized reinforcement:* Randi recognized that when Sam participated in learning activities he was more likely to continue to engage in that activity if she provided him with individualized reinforcement. Of course, she continued to use classwide reinforcement strategies, but knew that Sam preferred certain social and tactile reinforcements. For example, Sam enjoys squeezing a tacky ball. When Sam successfully participated in an activity, he was given the opportunity to squeeze the tacky ball. At the beginning of the year, Sam's teacher identified his preferred reinforcers and placed them in an easily accessible box.
- *Consult with specialists:* Sam's teacher consulted with the local school district's inclusion specialist to learn other strategies she could use with Sam to improve his ability to be an active member in her classroom. The specialist recommended two books that helped Sam's teacher in her daily dealings with Sam: (1) *Teaching Young Children With Autism Spectrum Disorder* by Clarissa Willis (2006) and (2) *Sensory Integration: A Guide for Preschool Teachers* by Christy Isbell and Rebecca Isbell (2007). In addition, Sam's teacher worked closely with a behavior specialist who assisted her in determining the cause of some behavioral outbursts that Sam was experiencing. She helped design an effective intervention plan to address the disruptive behaviors.

Table 3 defines characteristics teachers may observe when working with children with autism. Included in the table are ideas teachers can implement in response to the specific behavior addressed.

As children with autism progress into the elementary school ages, they may begin to experience potential difficulties directly related to academic instruction. Figure 4 identifies some of these potential difficulties and provides possible strategies that the teacher can use to address the specific area of difficulty.

Working With Families

Sam's teacher told Sam's family about the strategies she used in the classroom that they could use in their home to enhance his learning and development. Some specific strategies that families could do at home for a child with autism are:

Table 3
BEHAVIORS OBSERVED IN CHILDREN WITH AUTISM

What the Child Does	One's Natural Reaction	What the Teacher Should Do	*DSM-IV-TR* Characteristic of Autism
"Refuses" to answer questions	Go on to the next person and assume the child does not know the answer	Use simple language for questions; provide pictures and visual cues	Qualitative impairment in communication
Does not follow instructions	Consider the child noncompliant	Use gestures or sign language; pair the child with a peer	Qualitative impairment in communication
Does not look at teacher when being spoken to	Consider the child disrespectful	Make sure that you have the child's attention before speaking; establish a signal like raising the index finger before speaking	Lack of eye contact
Often has a blank look on his or her face during instruction	Assume the child is not learning	Assess learning using pictures, visual cues, choice making	Difficulty with nonverbal behaviors such as facial expression
Lacks friends	Assume that the child does not value others and does not want friends	Provide opportunities for positive peer interaction; peer learning activities	Lack of peer relationships at the child's developmental level
Is a loner on the playground and in the cafeteria	Assume the child prefers to be alone	Provide a lunch buddy for the cafeteria; promote interaction with socially adept peers	Lack of social reciprocity
Always talks about the same thing (e.g., dinosaurs or plumbing)	Remind the child that we are not talking about dinosaurs	Use the child's area of interest in instruction; pair the area of interest with other areas to expand repertoire of conversation	Restricted and repetitive patterns of interest and behavior
Flicking hands while looking at ceiling lights	Tell the child to stop or ask him why he is shaking his hands	Redirect the child and provide an activity involving hand movements	Repetitive movements
Cries or is aggressive when the routine changes	Tell the child to be quiet or send him to the office	Use a picture or visual schedule and warn of changes in routine	Adherence to routines

Note. From "Understanding Recommendations for Identification and Programming" (p. 18) by S. Lynch, 2009, in V. G. Spencer and C. G. Simpson (Eds.), *Teaching Children With Autism in the General Classroom*, Waco, TX: Prufrock Press Inc. Reprinted with permission.

♦ *Use a daily schedule*: Parents can develop a daily schedule with the child each morning and review it at the end of the day. We recommend creating schedules with pictures; in particular, photographs of the child completing the task or activity can be reinforcing.

Potential Difficulties	Possible Strategies
Student becomes overly agitated when testing or when other new situations are present	Identify a safe haven or relaxation area within the room or in another room, such as the library
Student feels overwhelmed by verbal interactions	Experiment more with written words, signing, or gestures
Student processes and follows instructions	Write instructions on board or have them written on the student's desk Use few words ("Sit at your desk") Repeat instructions one-on-one Allow extra time for processing Include pictures to accompany oral information
Student is unable to remain seated during instruction	Allow for frequent breaks but make sure the student knows what he is to be doing during the break and where it will occur
Student does not understand how long each activity requires	Set specific time limits for activities and use a Red Visual Timer to help the student understand the concept of time
Student answers open-ended questions	Structure the question to reduce confusion and choices
Student is reluctant to ask the teacher for help	Establish a special signal that indicates the student needs help. The teacher may learn the sign for the letter "H" and teach it to the student. When the student requires "help" he signs the letter "H"
Student does not have materials/ books for class	Use transparent zip folders for pens and pencils Use color-coded folders for each academic/subject area
Student refuses to enter specific rooms that may have sensory challenges: unusual smells or lighting (chemistry room, cafeteria)	Allow the student to take more frequent breaks
Student is unable to get started on work	Break the work into parts and use visuals to designate the work assignment
Student has difficulty starting/ completing homework	The student has spent a lot of energy making it through the day. How important is homework to this student? What are some different homework assignments that could be given that may address the student's interests?
Student is unable to complete work/ projects that develop over time	Use a written/visual planner that specifically lists the activity and date for completion of smaller assignments

FIGURE 4. Summary of areas of difficulty and possible strategies.

Note. Adapted from Kluth (2003), Ozonoff and Schetter (2007), and Simpson et al. (2003).

- *Teach choice making*: Parents should help their child make choices throughout the day (e.g., what to eat for snack, which toys to play with, whether to go to the park or to a library, selecting a book prior to bedtime). This builds competence in making decisions that can be carried over to the classroom.
- *Encourage the child to share*: By reminding their child about sharing and cooperating when he plays with siblings or with neighbors, parents can help reinforce preferred behaviors for the classroom.

- *Organize the space*: Parents should prepare visual boundaries (e.g., using carpet squares or small blankets) when the child is playing with puzzles or other toys. Items like playdough or snacks can be placed on baking sheets or plates with short rims so that children can see a visual boundary.
- *Develop social skills*: Creating social stories about activities that occur in their families (e.g., preparing a meal as a family, going to the grocery store, or getting ready for church or synagogue) can help parents model and reinforce ideal behaviors, especially for those activities that require specific conduct (i.e., quiet in the church or synagogue, washing one's hands when handling food). Role-playing the social stories with your child can be helpful, especially if family members show the child the actions they take within the activities.
- *Keep directions short:* Remind parents to limit directions for tasks at home to one or two steps and to check for understanding after each step.

SAFETY FIRST

Classroom safety is important for all children, but it especially is important when you have children in your classroom with autism. The following tips are critical to ensuring the safety of children with autism and all of the children in your classroom:
- Be prepared when out-of-the-ordinary events are planned for the day (such as a field trip, a special guest coming to visit the class, or someone bringing an animal to the classroom). A visitor to the classroom can disrupt children with autism, so plan to seat the child close to you so you can support him as you present novel activities.
- Remember that children with autism may be distracted easily. Keep the classroom door closed if the child has a history of wandering into other parts of the school or center.
- As children leave for the day, take the child with autism by the hand to ensure that he gets to his car or bus safely or walk close to him.

- If children are riding on a bus or in a van, supervise them as they get into the vehicle. A family member or guardian should be waiting at the bus stop nearest their home to help them get off the bus.

- Teach children about safety drills (e.g., fire or tornado). Before drills occur, take the time to practice ahead of time so that the child is used to the routine. Some children are oversensitive to sounds and this could cause agitation during safety drills. Comfort the child with autism so that he will not be overly frightened or overwhelmed when regular drills occur. Tell the children that "this is practice just in case we ever need to protect ourselves." When the drill is complete, continue to calm the children and reassure them that everything is OK.

IF YOU WANT TO KNOW MORE

Autism Research Institute
4182 Adams Avenue
San Diego, CA 92116
866-366-3361
http://www.autismresearchinstitute.com

Autism Society of America
7910 Woodmont Ave., Ste. 300
Bethesda, MD 20814-3067
301-657-0881 or 800-328-8476
http://www.autism-society.org

National Autism Association
1330 W. Schatz Lane
Nixa, MO 65714
877-622-2884
http://www.nationalautismassociation.org

National Dissemination Center for Children with Disabilities
1825 Connecticut Ave. NW, Ste. 700
Washington, DC 20009
800-695-0285
http://www.nichcy.org

National Institute of Child Health and Human Development
National Institutes of Health, DHHS
31 Center Drive, Rm. 2A32 MSC 2425
Bethesda, MD 20892-2425
800-370-2943
http://www.nichd.nih.gov

Effective Programming for Young Children With Autism (Ages 3–5)
http://www.specialed.us/autism/early/ear11.htm

CHAPTER 4

Robert

A CHILD WITH ATTENTION DEFICIT/
HYPERACTIVITY DISORDER (ADHD)

When Robert came to Ms. Jana's classroom on the first day of school, his mother told Jana that he had been diagnosed with ADHD. "He takes prescribed daily medication, so his behavior should be much like the other children in his class. Let me know if you have any problems," she explained to Jana. "We want his classroom experience to be as positive as possible."

Robert was a delightful child, full of life and eager to enjoy the opportunities that Ms. Jana's classroom offered. Jana recognized from the very beginning that he was intelligent and curious about everything going on around him. Most of Robert's classroom hours were uneventful, although he often exhibited jittery and excitable behavior. He always seemed to be in the middle of classroom activity, and some of his quieter peers preferred playing with others because of Robert's rambunctious approach to his learning experiences.

Occasionally, Robert would become disruptive, especially during Circle Time. He had difficulty sitting still for even brief periods of time—usually only about 3 or 4 minutes—and normal discussion in a group setting was almost impossible for him, while most of his peers were able to attend for 10 minutes or more. He would blurt out answers to questions and did not understand the give and take that group discussions require. Even Jana's attempts to call on other children in the group were ignored as Robert, eager to become the center of attention, kept talking, sometimes endlessly. If Robert's mother forgot to give him his medication, Robert's behavior deteriorated to the point that he would throw temper tantrums and cry loudly if classroom events weren't going the way he wanted. These days were difficult for Jana and the entire group to manage.

OVERVIEW OF ATTENTION DEFICIT/HYPERACTIVITY DISORDER

ADHD is a very common childhood disorder that has rapidly gained attention over the last decade. Currently, as many as 3.8 million school-age children are said to have ADHD. The National Institute of Mental Health (2006) estimated that ADHD occurs in 3% to 5% of preschoolers and school-age children. Children with ADHD can face long-term problems within their homes, schools, and the community.

Much debate exists over the causes and treatment of ADHD. Many causes of ADHD have been identified; however, these causes often are misunderstood by teachers and families of children diagnosed with ADHD. The causes of ADHD may include genetics (ADHD often is hereditary) and environmental influences (toxins, such as lead). Findings show that ADHD is a neurobiological condition. Specifically, studies have found that the part of the brain that controls or regulates impulses, attention, and behavior is thought to be underactive when compared to children without ADHD (Pfiffner, 1996). Although these causes often are associated with ADHD, the exact cause of ADHD is unknown.

The primary symptoms of ADHD are hyperactivity, impulsivity, and inattention. A child exhibiting *hyperactivity* in the classroom might touch things frequently, wiggle her hands and feet, and play with surrounding objects. In general, this child is in constant motion, moving from place to place, shifting her body, and touching items in the environment. The definition of inattentiveness is "failure to pay attention." A child who is *inattentive* often gets bored with something she is doing, is distracted easily, has problems following directions, and forgets to write things down (this specifically occurs in older children).

The last symptom of ADHD is *impulsivity*. Impulsivity occurs when a child tends to act without thinking through a situation. Often this action occurs in bursts or in response to an emotion. A child exhibiting impulsivity may have a hard time waiting in line or taking turns when playing a game. She also may have a difficult time holding back her feelings and emotions.

When diagnosing a child, a psychologist, psychiatrist, or physician would refer to the *DSM-IV-TR* manual (APA, 2000), which includes information about mental health disorders. Both mental health providers and medical professionals use the manual to aid in making a variety of diagnoses within their specific fields. Professionals refer to this book when seeking information regarding diagnoses and treatment options for numerous disorders. A professional might examine several characteristics of ADHD, such as:

- squirming,
- difficulty remaining seated,
- blurting out answers,
- fidgeting,
- difficulty paying and sustaining attention,
- talking excessively,
- difficulty playing quietly,
- interrupting or being rude to others, and
- difficulty waiting for turns.

It is important to note that all children, even those who are typically developing, tend to display many of the characteristics above. This leads to a great deal of difficulty in making an actual diagnosis in young children. "Children with ADHD display extremes in these behaviors and often appear to have no control over them" (Rutledge, 2008, p. 4).

Along with a few additional characteristics, a professional would look to see if specific characteristics such as those listed previously are present. In addition, in order for a medical professional to make an actual diagnosis of ADHD, a child's symptoms must be present before the age of 7 and should continue for a period of no less than 6 months.

Also, the symptoms must affect at least two areas of the child's life. For example, if a child is overly active at school, but not at home, church, or the babysitter's house, she would more than likely not have ADHD but rather a behavior as the result of something occurring within the school setting. Professionals also determine if a parent or sibling has ADHD. If so, the likelihood of a child exhibiting the above listed symptoms associated with ADHD increases.

The National Institute of Mental Health (2006) stated that

> specialists consider several critical questions when assessing a child for ADHD: Are these behaviors excessive, long-term and pervasive? That is, do they occur more often than in other children that same age? Are they a continuous problem, not just a response to a temporary situation? Do the behaviors occur in several settings or only in one specific place like the playground or in the schoolroom? The person's pattern of behavior is compared against a set of criteria and characteristics of the disorder as listed in the DSM-IV-TR. (p. 7)

Some teachers and parents are unaware that there are three types of ADHD: ADHD predominantly inattentive type, ADHD predominantly hyperactive type, and ADHD mixed. Children with ADHD predominantly inattentive type often do not exhibit the hyperactive component. Unfortunately, specialists sometimes overlook the diagnosis of this type of ADHD because the hyperactivity component is not prevalent.

A child with ADHD predominantly inattentive type might look as though she is paying attention in class. In reality, the child is not focusing on what is front of her but is instead daydreaming or thinking of something happening outside of school. A child with ADHD predominantly hyperactive type is easier to identify because the hyperactivity component is apparent and the child often disrupts the activities taking place around him.

WHAT TEACHERS NEED TO KNOW ABOUT ADHD

The likelihood of children in your preschool classroom being diagnosed with ADHD is limited, but not nonexistent. Many teachers and family members are quick to assume that a child has ADHD if he is easily distracted or not able to finish tasks. The reality is that many children and adults without ADHD exhibit these same characteristics.

Diagnosing ADHD in toddlers and preschoolers can present a challenge because many typically developing 3- to 5-year-old children exhibit the same characteristics of ADHD within their normal developmental patterns. Children under the age of 5 rarely receive diagnoses of ADHD because a high activity level is a normal childhood behavior in toddlers and preschoolers. Children within this age range often are captivated by one thing and often only for a limited time. A short attention span in a typically developing child is to be expected. However, if a child seems to have an endless amount of activity that is not focused or goal-directed, it warrants further investigation.

You probably realize that all children have times when their behaviors seem unacceptable. Toddlers especially are likely to communicate their feelings and frustrations through outbursts. Many times the outbursts stem from outside sources, such as sleepiness, hunger, or sickness. Regardless of the reason, such outbursts tend to disrupt the daily schedule.

A child with ADHD may experience these outbursts more frequently. As in many situations, creating collaborative relationships with families is essential in reducing those negative behaviors associated with ADHD. Families should be encouraged to keep open the lines of communication between teachers and other professionals involved with the child during the school day. Involving families in tasks such as monitoring behaviors at home and reporting them to you, or reinforcing a child through verbal praise for taking turns at home can be of great assistance in teaching the child to generalize newly learned skills.

It also is important to realize that a child with ADHD may want to participate in classroom activities, but the child's impulsivity and inattentiveness may be interfering with her ability to do so. You should consider this information when responding to a child's actions. You also should be aware that the same inattentiveness and hyperactivity that disrupts classroom instruction also might have a direct impact on a child's family life, as well as her ability to create and maintain friendships.

A child with ADHD will need support from you to help her complete tasks, pay attention, develop peer relationships, and follow directions. The next section identifies several teaching strategies to help you support children with ADHD.

As a teacher, it is important to be aware of the various treatment options that are available to children with ADHD. More and more frequently, children with ADHD receive treatment through a variety of medications including stimulants and nonstimulants. Medication for children with ADHD has shown to improve their attention and focus. It is a common misconception that stimulants and nonstimulants cure ADHD. In fact, this is clearly not the case. Medications for ADHD should help to control the symptoms of ADHD. New and improved medications offer the child the opportunity to take medication in a single dose that lasts throughout the day.

Although physicians frequently prescribe medications to control symptoms of ADHD, physicians also recommend that children take medication only with other types of support, such as social skills training; cognitive training (typically short-term psychotherapy focusing on how the individual thinks, behaves, and communicates at the given time of therapy rather than on past events); support groups for families; and behavior modification (see the "Attention Deficit/Hyperactivity Disorder: Inclusive Classroom Strategies" section on pp. 67–74). Social skill training and behavior modification are two elements of a treatment plan that teachers can incorporate into the child's daily routine.

Children with ADHD need clearly defined behavioral expectations. Reward systems that offer immediate feedback typically are very effective. Focusing on a child's positive attributes through praise will help the child develop a more positive self-esteem. Social skills training can involve simple activities such as role-playing how to stand in line or taking turns to identify emotions and feelings through facial expressions. As you begin to collaborate with families, various roles and responsibilities will be defined.

If a child in your classroom is taking medication, it is important for you to report to the family how the child is responding to the medication. Does the child seem to be eating less? Are the child's activity levels increasing throughout the day? Has her personality drastically changed? This type of information is important to the family or guardian so they can tell their physician. Many families decide that medication is not an appropriate treatment option for their child. Although a child may not take medication, teachers, families, or caregivers must still work on addressing those behaviors that occur within the school day.

Unfortunately, ADHD generates a great deal of negative expectations. However, research shows that many children with ADHD possess gifts that contribute to their success across settings. Honos-Webb (2005) identified five such gifts: creativity, exuberance, emotional sensitivity, interpersonal intuition, and increased ecological consciousness. In searching various Web sites, families, teachers, and other professionals in the field have created informal lists of those strengths that some children with ADHD possess. These lists include characteristics such as being extremely creative, imaginative, enthusiastic, and hard working, and having an ability to multitask. In today's society, it can be easy to forget what wonderful characteristics these are for a child to have! When learning to embrace the strengths of a child with ADHD, remember that some historians believe that both Albert Einstein and Thomas Edison had ADHD, and each day individuals can find evidence of the contributions those two great thinkers made to society. When working with children with ADHD in the class-room setting, find a place for children to "show off" the strengths they have and utilize available modifications and accommodations.

Most importantly, a teacher should be very familiar with the child's IFSP or IEP. Knowing the specific needs of the child and the responsibilities of those team members involved in his or her plan is essential in creating a successful program. Working collaboratively with families, professionals, and other caregivers will provide consistency for the child.

ATTENTION DEFICIT/HYPERACTIVITY DISORDER: INCLUSIVE CLASSROOM STRATEGIES

Children with ADHD may display some of the same characteristics that children with autism have. You may want to reread Chapter 3 (Sam: A Child With Autism Spectrum Disorder) to gain insight about helping children who have ADHD.

Family Interventions

Families who have children with ADHD may experience higher levels of stress than families with typically developing children. A look at the statistics reflecting the implications that ADHD has on families is alarming. For example, "divorce rates in families where a child has ADD occurs three times more frequently than in the general population, and 50–75 percent of incarcerated inmates in prisons have some form of ADD" (Lawlis, 2005, p. 13). In addition, research indicates that attention disorders tend to run in families and genetics are likely to influence the presence of ADHD. Studies show that "relatives of clinically referred ADD children and adolescents have a significantly increased risk for ADD" (Biederman, Faraone, Keenen, Knee, & Tsuang, 1990, p. 531). Specifically, children who have a parent with ADHD have a greater than 50% chance of having ADHD themselves (Biederman et al., 1995).

Another stress inducer is that children with ADHD may have difficult temperaments, making their characteristics persistent and sometimes quite serious. These families often seek out help for their children. It is important to remind families of children with ADHD that while "there's no treatment approach that works for all children, there are strategies that do work and that can be combined to create an effective program for their child" (Lawlis, 2005, p. 11).

PARTNERING WITH PARENTS

Having a cooperative relationship with families of children with ADHD will help as those families struggle with their children's impulsivity and hyperactivity. Regularly communicate with families about the strategies you are using in the classroom that they can use at home with their child. If you and the family make a concerted effort to teach the child with ADHD how to manage his behavior and improve his social relationships, then strategies become more valuable to the child.

Share any information you have regarding support groups for families of children with ADHD, if you are aware of any in your area. You also could organize a support group for families of children who have ADHD. Another way to help families is to provide them with a list of resources that they can contact to find support (see the section titled "If You Want to Know More" at the end of this chapter).

Classroom Interventions

It is important for teachers of children with ADHD to have patience and a good understanding of various strategies to use to keep the children focused and attentive to learning. Children with ADHD may benefit from having a paraeducator or teacher's aide in the classroom (but this is not always necessary for the child to be successful). A second person in the classroom can help the child acquire social skills and learn how to join play settings.

DEMONSTRATE SPECIFIC SKILLS AND TASKS

It is important for a child with ADHD to clearly understand the information that is presented to him. Teachers should take time to model and demonstrate specific skills and instructions in the most concrete method possible. The use of hands-on materials and real-life experiences can assist teachers in demonstrating skills and tasks.

Behavior Modification

Most early childhood professionals resist behavior modification techniques when working with young children because of its emphasis on external motivation and lack of opportunities for children to develop independent self-management strategies. Nevertheless, these behavioral strategies help children with ADHD achieve self-management and self-discipline when they are applied appropriately and consistently.

Having a plan of action means that you are *aware* of problems that may occur, know *when* the behaviors are likely to occur, have a *strategy* for solving the problems, and are prepared to *implement* the plan. For example, if a child with ADHD usually has an outburst when she goes into the Block Center, you might use this plan of action:

- Talk to the child before she enters the center and remind her that appropriate behavior is expected.
- Explain what the appropriate behavior is and how she should behave.
- Monitor her play in the Block Center.
- Remove her if her play becomes behaviorally unacceptable.
- Give her further instructions about calming herself.
- Let her enter the center again if she agrees to demonstrate acceptable behavior.
- Praise the child when she demonstrates appropriate behavior.
- If she is unable to demonstrate appropriate behavior, remove her again and redirect her play to another center choice.
- Tell the child that she can try another time (or another day) in the Block Center.

Social Skills Training

All children in early childhood classrooms need to learn how to get along with one another. The skills that socialization requires include understanding another's viewpoint, negotiating for desired objects (specific toys or opportunities to play in certain centers), comprehending how to participate in a democratic culture, knowing how to take turns, and cooperating with others. It is important to use part of your curriculum activities to teach the children in your class each of these skills.

Teaching social skills to a child with ADHD requires greater individualization, and the training becomes situation specific. For example, if a child with ADHD wants a snack, he may just take it, whether it belongs to him or to someone else. Use the specific situation to talk about alternative behaviors. ("If you want another cracker, ask for it" or "The plate of crackers in the middle of the table is for those who want another one. Take one of those crackers instead of grabbing Delton's cracker.")

Plan social skills training as part of your daily lessons and take advantage of opportunities for additional instruction that are also spontaneous and unplanned. Use the child's behaviors to help you teach her to become socially adept. Always remember to:

- monitor children's social interactions;
- ignore minor problems;
- teach children in small groups, if possible;
- use individualized instruction;
- praise children when they demonstrate appropriate behaviors; and
- acknowledge children when they participate in classroom activities (this particularly will be true during Circle Time lessons; Turnbull et al., 2007).

As with all young children, developing social skills takes time—becoming socialized does not occur overnight. Be prepared to teach the same skills repeatedly, especially for children with ADHD.

Understanding Tactile Defensiveness

Some children with ADHD have hypersensitive responses to routine tactile stimulation (Parush, Sohmer, Steinberg, & Kaitz, 2007). This response to tactile stimulation often is referred to as tactile defensiveness. Lightsey (1993) found that a strong relationship exists between tactile defensiveness and ADHD. These findings were very similar to another study conducted by Huecker and Kinnealey (1998).

In the preschool classroom, children with tactile defensiveness may respond negatively when touching objects found in their environments. A child might recoil if she is expected to use playdough or finger paint, and may not like touching rough or gritty surfaces. Just as some people respond negatively to loud noises or bright lights, some children are more sensitive to tactile objects. Knowing this aspect of children's behavior will help you to ease some of the classroom problems that the child with ADHD might have.

It is important not to force a child who is tactile defensive into a situation where she has to engage with an object that produces a hypersensitive response. Additional information specifically addressing children's sensory needs can be found in a book by Christy Isbell and Rebecca Isbell (2007) called *Sensory Integration: A Guide for Preschool Teachers*.

Using Play

Children with ADHD need increased opportunities for active physical play. Typically developing children are energetic, but as they move through their daily routines and interact with others, they become tired by the end of the day. This usually is not the case for children with ADHD. Plan opportunities for children to have frequent active play times. In all natural settings (home and school), children need to participate in active physical play experiences. Whenever possible, take the children outside to the playground to get the physical activity that they need!

Applying the Strategies

> Robert would become disruptive, especially during Circle Time. He had difficulty sitting still for even brief periods—usually only about 3 or 4 minutes—and normal discussion in a group setting was almost impossible for him. He would blurt out answers to questions and did not understand the give and take that group discussions require.

Jana, Robert's teacher, had attended workshops about ADHD, so she had some insight about what to expect from Robert's participation in her classroom. As a general rule, she was an encouraging teacher and her positive attitude toward Robert was critical to his transition into her group. She quickly assessed her classroom environment and then developed a set of plans that she thought she could use to accommodate Robert's needs as a learner. The following are some of the strategies his teacher used.

Working With the Whole Class

Robert's teacher incorporated the following strategies for behaviors and techniques that would affect her entire class.

- *Post a visual daily schedule*: Jana posted a visual daily schedule for all of the children in her classroom. She posted it at Robert's eye level so that she could prepare him for the day's activities. The visual schedule paired with a verbal prompt such as, "Now, we're getting ready for lunch. See this picture of children eating—that reminds us that it's time for us to have lunch," helped Robert follow a structured routine.

- *Foster friendships*: Preschool teachers help children develop friendships with their classmates. Fortunately for Jana, her class included several fairly active boys. They accepted Robert easily and they played together well, especially on the playground. Occasionally, when Robert's behavior became too rambunctious, she would step in quickly to assist group members in helping Robert "slow down" and "be calm." These boys were important to Robert because their peer support became instructional as they modeled ways to control their own behavior.

- *Help with group projects*: If children participated in a group project (e.g., making a fire truck out of a large refrigerator box), Jana helped Robert determine what he could do to help. She gave him specific, short directions about how to engage actively in the group work. She helped Robert by supplying the necessary materials to complete the project. All of the other materials were removed to limit Robert's opportunity for distraction.

- *Maintain consistency*: As the school year progressed, Robert needed far less of Jana's attention. Because she maintained consistency in her classroom furniture arrangement and her normal interactions with him, Robert began to demonstrate more independence. She monitored him carefully, because she knew that at any moment, the level of support Robert needed might change.

WORKING WITH INDIVIDUAL CHILDREN

Robert's teacher used the following strategies in working with him one-on-one:

- *Keep the child close*: Jana kept Robert as close to her throughout the day as possible, especially during Circle Time. Seating the child close to her during group experiences helped him focus on what he should be learning instead of being distracted by other children. Using physical touch also was helpful in encouraging Robert to continue to work on the tasks presented to him.

- *Maintain good eye contact and praise good behavior*: When Jana interacted with Robert, she made sure she maintained good eye contact with him. When he appeared to be attentive or if he answered a question, she praised his behavior. Jana was sure to have Robert look directly at her face when she was speaking.

- *Prepare the child for transitions*: When transitions were necessary (moving to Center Time, for example, or leaving the room to go outdoors), Jana always forewarned Robert what was about to happen. She alerted him a few minutes before changing activities that something new was about to happen. The use of verbal cues and reminders was helpful to Robert. Often Jana would have Robert repeat the direction before moving on to the next transition step.

- *Help the child monitor his own behavior*: Jana often talked to Robert about monitoring his own behavior. If she saw that he was becoming frustrated, she would get down at his eye level and say, "Robert, tell yourself to be calm. Stay calm, Robert. Just tell yourself to be calm." When he complied, she complimented him on his ability to manage his own behavior, saying, "It's great when you can tell yourself to be calm. Keep saying that to yourself when you feel like stomping your feet or yelling."

- *Offer limited choices*: Jana limited Robert's choices for centers: For example, she gave him choices such as, "You can go to the Science Table or to the Grocery Store Center—which do you prefer?" When he participated with manipulatives, she offered only two or three options for him (e.g., stringing beads, playing with attribute blocks, or putting a puzzle together). Jana learned early in the year that Robert would react negatively when he became overwhelmed, and she planned carefully to keep this from happening. She also gave him the choice to sit or stand while engaging in center activities.

- *Give one instruction at a time*: Jana also learned that Robert could not manage more than one instruction or directive at a time. She took the time to tell him what he needed to do next and repeated the instructions, if necessary. She was careful to get down to Robert's physical height level when she spoke to him. This strategy allowed Robert to focus his attention on his teacher's directions. Often, if Jana was discussing a specific item or object, she would hold that object directly in front of her when she spoke about it.

WORKING WITH FAMILIES

Teachers of children with ADHD can use these strategies Robert's teacher employed to work with families:

- *Communicate positive techniques with families*: Jana talked with Robert's family about positive techniques that they could use at home to encourage good behavior. Among her suggestions were to maintain good eye contact with Robert and to talk to him often, praise his good behavior, prepare him for transitions (e.g., going to the mall, getting ready for bed), help Robert monitor his own behavior, offer one or two choices, and give him only one instruction at a time. Once a week she called Robert's mother for a conversation that was mutually beneficial to them both.
- *Research the condition*: Jana continued to read everything she could find about ADHD and attended workshops as they became available to her. She used the Internet as well and searched for organizations that would help her and Robert's family understand more about his condition, as well as suggest ways they could help him. (See the section at the end of the chapter "If You Want to Know More" to learn about some of the Web sites that Jana thought were helpful.)
- *Give rewards:* Jana encouraged Robert's parents to provide social or physical rewards for Robert's efforts to pay attention and listen at home.
- *Focus on positives:* Jana reminded his parents that when Robert engaged in inappropriate behaviors they should tell him what to do correctly and not focus on what he did wrong.

SAFETY FIRST

When teachers have children in their classrooms with ADHD, the following tips are critical to ensuring their safety:

- Be prepared when out-of-the-ordinary events are planned for the day (e.g., a field trip, a special guest coming in, someone bringing in an animal). A visitor to the classroom can disrupt children with ADHD, so plan to seat them close to you so you can hold them close if necessary.

- Remember that children with ADHD are easily distracted. Keep the classroom door closed to prevent them from wandering into other parts of the school or center. You may even need a latch above children's reach to prevent them from leaving the classroom.

- If an aide or volunteer is unavailable to help in the classroom, have a backup plan for the times the child has an extreme outburst (e.g., you might take her to the director's or principal's office until she is calm enough to return to your classroom).

- As children leave for the day, take the child with ADHD by the hand and escort him to the appropriate car or bus.

- If the child with ADHD is riding on a bus (or in a van), supervise her as she gets into the vehicle. A family member should be waiting at the bus stop nearest their home to help the child get off the bus.

- Teach children about safety drills (e.g., fire or tornado). Explain that "this is practice just in case we ever need to protect ourselves." Many children with ADHD are not easily calmed when safety drills and emergencies occur. If possible, hold the child close to you, but keep in mind that this procedure may not prevent a tantrum or outburst.

- Reduce clutter and external stimuli. These items can distract a child from paying attention in class, but they also can distract a child during an emergency situation.

IF YOU WANT TO KNOW MORE

CHADD National Office
8181 Professional Place, Ste. 150
Landover, MD 20785
301-306-7070
http://www.CHADD.org

LD OnLine
WETA Public Television
2775 S. Quincy St.
Arlington, VA 22206
http://www.ldonline.org/indepth/adhd

National Dissemination Center for Children with Disabilities
1825 Connecticut Ave. NW, Ste. 700
Washington, DC 20009
800-695-0285
http://www.nichcy.org

National Resource Center on ADHD (Sponsored by CHADD)
http://help4adhd.org

ADHD Information Resources
http://www.adhdnews.com/states.htm

CHAPTER 5

Andrew

A CHILD WITH A SPEECH
OR LANGUAGE IMPAIRMENT

When Andrew arrived in Mr. Neuwirth's prekindergarten classroom, he was almost nonverbal. Mr. Neuwirth realized early in the school year that Andrew's communication would be difficult for her to understand, and throughout the year he struggled to interpret his responses and communication during group work and in his individual contact with him. Andrew mumbled most of the time and his rare comments were only a few words long, much more typical of a 2-year-old child than a 4-year-old child in prekindergarten.

Andrew's classmates enjoyed being around him, and many of them wanted to play with him in the Home Living Center. His willingness to do what they asked of him allowed him to take on the role of baby in each encounter when children were playing "house." Andrew was almost like a doll they played with, except that he was alive.

Mr. Neuwirth's attempts to understand Andrew's language were limited by his own understanding of speech and language impairments, so he contacted the school district's speech-language pathologist to determine what type of assistance Andrew needed. He had suspected that he might have a hearing impairment, but the speech-language pathologist would be better qualified to make this diagnosis and chart a course of action to improve his language.

He also learned from Andrew's mother that he had been in a serious car accident when he was very young, and he began to suspect that this might be part of his problem. He was hopeful that the speech-language pathologist would be able to identify the type of speech and language problems Andrew demonstrated—surely help was available for this young child whose educational experiences were hampered by language and perhaps other developmental delays.

OVERVIEW OF SPEECH OR LANGUAGE IMPAIRMENTS

Many young children enrolled in childcare facilities may have received speech or language impairment diagnoses at an early age. These children may enter your center or preschool with an identifying diagnosis of language delay. Language delay is a term often used when a child

> exhibits typical development in all areas except language. The development of language in a child with a language delay is believed to follow the same patterns seen in children with typical language development; however the development of language is protracted, with the child reaching the same milestones at a slower rate. (Raver, 2009, p. 117)

Often children with language delays are monitored during therapy and if, as they become older, the delays continue, a diagnosis of language impairment is established.

Children with suspected speech and/or language impairments (including those suspected of a language delay) should be evaluated by speech-language pathologists. Often a speech-language pathologist is referred to as a speech therapist, speech pathologist, or a speech clinician. The American Speech-Language-Hearing Association (ASHA) prefers the term speech-language pathologist, as it is more reflective of the orientation of the profession. In order to assist a speech-language pathologist in properly diagnosing and providing services to children with speech and/or language impairments, it is imperative that teachers understand the complexity in defining a speech or language disorder. Speech and language impairments may exist together, or a child may have a delay in speech or language only. Often we hear the words *communication*, *speech*, and *language* used interchangeably. It is important to note that these terms are very different and address specific elements of development.

"Speech is the system of forming and producing sounds that are the basis of language" (Mastropieri & Scruggs, 2007, p. 52). When considering this definition, speech impairment would be a disorder that affects the spoken language. There are several types of speech impairments, including stuttering, aphasia (inability to produce or comprehend language), articulation disorders, or a speech impairment related to a hearing impairment. The causes for speech impairments are, for the most part, unknown, but, in some cases, impairments are caused by growths, infections, or trauma to the larynx; infections of the tonsils, adenoid glands, or sinuses; or physical impairments (Mastropieri & Scruggs, 2007). Physical impairments may involve cleft lip or palate. Many children with hearing loss also exhibit speech and/or language impairments. Regardless of the specific cause of the speech impairment, it can impact a child's social, academic, and occupational success; therefore, early detection is key to helping these children (Keating, Ozanne, & Turrell, 2005).

One common childhood speech impairment mentioned above is stuttering. Stuttering is a specific communication disorder

> characterized by disruptions in the forward flow of speech (or "speech disfluency"), such as repetitions of whole words or parts of words, prolongations of sounds, or complete blockages of sound. Speech disfluencies can be accompanied by physical tension or struggle, though many young children do not exhibit such tension in the early stages. (Coleman, Yaruss, & Hammer, 2004, p. 1)

It often is difficult to distinguish between normal disfluency (e.g., stuttering) and a true speech impairment. However, speech-language pathologists will evaluate many factors including "how often a child stutters and in what way" (Hamaguchi, 2001, p. 62). The pathologist often will "observe the child in a number of situations and takes careful notes as to how many time this child exhibits stuttering behaviors; the therapist also notes whether the child shows frustration" (Hamaguchi, 2001, p. 63). There does not seem be a specific cause for stuttering but it is suggested that stuttering has a psychological or physical basis.

As previously mentioned, the terms *speech* and *communication* often are used interchangeably. To further clarify this misuse, consider the following:

> While individuals use primarily speech for the purpose of communication, it is not the only way to communicate. Writing, signing, text messaging, and even drawing are other modes of communication. The communication mode selected depends on the abilities of the speaker. (Raver, 2009, p. 116)

Children with significant speech disorders may benefit from the use of alternative or augmentative communication devices to assist in communication.

A language disorder is an impairment that directly interferes with a child's ability to understand language (receptive), or to speak what one intends to say (expressive), or both. The American Speech-Language-Hearing Association (ASHA, 1982) defined language disorders as:

> An impairment in the comprehension and use of spoken, written or other symbol system. The disorder may involve the form of language (morphology, phonology, and syntax), the content of language (semantic system), and/or the function of language communication (pragmatic system) in any combination. (pp. 949–950)

As previously mentioned, speech and language impairments can coexist, or an individual may demonstrate only one impairment. This also holds true with the type of language impairment that a child exhibits. Young children and toddlers with both expressive and receptive language impairments (see Table 4) commonly are identified as having a language developmental impairment. A child with an expressive language impairment may not be able to formulate the appropriate utterances, but may be able to clearly understand what is said to him (e.g., hearing and following directions). Table 4 provides a list of the differences between speech impairments and language impairments.

Although a classroom teacher, childcare provider, or childcare director would not be in a position to diagnose a speech and/or language impairment, a childcare professional could gather relevant information through interactions and observations that may be helpful for a

Table 4
SPEECH VERSUS LANGUAGE IMPAIRMENT

	Definition	Impairment Indicators
Speech	Production of sounds, including factors such as vocal quality, rate of speaking, and articulation. Specifically, it is the mechanics of talking.	Occurs when a child or individual omits, distorts, substitutes, stutters, or has a hoarse vocal quality.
Language	The use of symbols that give meaning to speech (e.g., the use of words, gestures, or sign language to communicate). Language typically is referred to in two forms: expressive (ability to understand what is heard and seen) and receptive (ability to express oneself through speaking, gestures, or written words).	Often indicated when a child has difficulty asking and responding to questions, difficulty understanding written language (i.e., what is read), inability to recall and follow directions, and use of poor sentence structure.

Note. Adapted from Overton (2008).

speech-language pathologist to use in accurately diagnosing and treating this disability. A speech-language pathologist uses an array of assessments to accurately diagnose a specific impairment in a child. Often the speech-language pathologist will use parent questionnaires (which frequently are administered to caregivers as well), play-based assessments, communication-based assessments, language samples, and comprehension assessments.

Specific assessments that may be used include Sequenced Inventory of Communicative Development (Hendrick, Prather, & Tobin, 1984), Clinical Evaluation of Language Fundamentals-Preschool (CELF-P; Wig, Semel, & Secord, 2004), Preschool Language Scales (PLS; Zimmerman, Steiner, & Pond, 2002), Peabody Picture Vocabulary Test (PPVT; Dunn & Dunn, 1997). In addition, a therapist may include a criterion-referenced assessment such as the Assessment of Phonological Process, Revised (Hodson, 1986). Several types of assessments are available and a trained therapist will select the assessments based on the specific needs of the child being assessed.

As previously mentioned, the causes of speech and language delays are not fully known. Some researchers have identified possible causes such as sensory integration issues, congenital conditions, bilingual speech and language issues, brain injury, lip and/or tongue muscle weaknesses, mouth breathing, seizure disorders, restricted tissue under the tongue, abuse and neglect, and fluctuating hearing loss from middle ear fluid (Hamaguchi, 2001). If a child has a significant delay in speech and language it may impact him or her academically. Keeping this in mind, it is important that early identification and intervention occur. The earlier that a delay is detected, the more likely intervention will occur.

WHAT TEACHERS NEED TO KNOW ABOUT SPEECH OR LANGUAGE IMPAIRMENTS

You should be aware that many children with speech or language impairments are diagnosed prior to entering your classroom. However, a few children may have unidentified speech and/or language impairments. Families typically are the first to suspect that a child may have a speech or language impairment and often bring their concerns to the classroom teacher. As a teacher or caregiver, it is essential to listen to the family's concerns and begin to keep a watchful eye for specific indications that the child may indeed need speech or language screening by a speech-language pathologist. Children learn language and communication skills more efficiently prior to age 5. However, this does not mean that a child older than age 5 will not develop language skills. It is important to reinforce communication skills, which lay the foundation for a more positive educational experience. Early intervention and detection will help foster the acquisition of language and assist in building communication skills when children are young. "Early intervention is critical because language development affects the development of cognitive and social-emotional skills" (Dunlap, 2008, p. 152).

SUMMARY OF LANGUAGE DEVELOPMENT

Family members and teachers often search for charts of guidelines that indicate typical language development. Use developmental charts with caution and never use them to diagnose a speech and/or language impairment. Professionals trained in this area should make diagnoses. However, developmental charts can play a role in helping both teachers and parents in monitoring a child's growth and development (see box for helpful guidelines in language development).

Unlike an expressive language impairment (see box), a receptive language impairment focuses on a child's ability to understand, not

A GUIDE TO UNDERSTANDING LANGUAGE DEVELOPMENT

The following information indicates specific milestones in two age categories, in reference to sound productions, that children in the preschool setting reach and the age in which they occur. The sound productions are based on the milestones that 75–90% of children in each age group are capable of producing.

- From 3 ½–4 years, most preschoolers will clearly articulate *b, d, k, g, f,* and *y* (Feit, 2007).
- From 5–7 years, most children will articulate *t, ing, r, l,* and the voiceless *th, ch, sh,* and *j.* In addition, they will have mastered *f, v, sh, zh, th,* and *l* (Feit, 2007).

Indicators that a child may have a language impairment may be more difficult to spot because the child might not have an expressive language impairment. In addition, an articulation disorder does not indicate that a child will always have a language impairment. Some early warning signs of difficulties with verbal expression are the child's:

- inability or difficulty in naming items around him (e.g., he cannot retrieve the word he is looking for when trying to name an item);
- misnaming of specific items (giving the wrong name to an item);
- confusion of the use of grammatical rules;
- use of immature grammatical patterns, such as "me go" or "him good;" and
- difficulty with developing vocabulary or determining word meaning (semantics).

Additionally, a basic guideline for you to follow when determining if a child needs additional screening for an expressive language impairment is as follows:

- From age 3–4 years, the child is only intelligible to strangers 50% of the time and only uses short, simple sentences. Also, determine if the child has trouble expressing his ideas and doesn't sing familiar songs (Feit, 2007).
- From 4–5 years, the child makes errors in producing consonants such as *b, p, d, t, k, m, n, r, l, w,* and *s.* Also, determine if the child doesn't answer simple questions such as what, who, why, and how many (Feit, 2007).
- From 5–7 years, the child does not tell familiar stories or talk about his feelings (Feit, 2007).

There are a variety of resources available that publish materials directly related to speech and language development. A link to these resources is available at the American Speech-Language-Hearing Association Web site (http://www.asha.org).

speak, the language. Frequently, you may confuse a language impairment with a behavior issue or noncompliance in the classroom. This can be seen more clearly when looking at the signs of a receptive language impairment. Some children with receptive language impairments have a difficult time responding to questions requiring "yes" or "no" answers. They also often struggle with who, what, when, where, and why and how questions.

Another sign of a receptive language impairment is what is referred to as echolalia. This occurs when a child repeats words and phrases that are spoken, either immediately after they are spoken or at a later time. Many children with receptive language delays are unable to follow directions or routines, may not attend to spoken language, or may use jargon or predesigned responses (memorized answers or phrases). Your observation of all children will help the family in making decisions about speech and hearing screening.

Regardless of whether a child has already been identified with or simply shows signs of a speech and/or language impairment, constant communication and collaboration with families and therapists (speech-language pathologists) is key to a successful intervention plan. Both parents and professionals can implement the strategies provided.

SPEECH OR LANGUAGE IMPAIRMENTS: INCLUSIVE LEARNING STRATEGIES

Family Interventions

When children have speech or language impairments, teachers, families, and speech-language pathologists need to work together to improve children's opportunities to interact with others, participate in play settings, and develop friendships with classmates and peers outside the family group. With appropriate intervention, most children will begin to make progress toward overcoming the specific speech and or language impairment addressed. The severity of the impairment and the amount of progress a child makes in therapy will determine the future prognosis. Family members also can help develop early language skills by (Hamaguchi, 2001):

- reading to their children on a daily basis,

- discouraging baby talk,
- avoiding allowing siblings to speak for a younger child,
- praising any attempt at speaking,
- encouraging communication by talking with their child frequently,
- responding to their child's questions by offering complete answers,
- talking about the events that are taking place and actions you are performing, and
- using rhyming words and games to help children learn about words and sounds.

In addition, families and caregivers should recognize that specific actions could hinder language development, such as allowing others to tease or make fun of a child with a specific speech or language impairment, interrupting a child when he speaks, withholding objects from a child to make him speak, insisting that the child repeat words, and placing any unnecessary demands on the child (e.g., speaking in front of groups; Dunlap, 2008). These actions should be avoided. Sharing this information with those who interact with the child will prove beneficial in the child's success.

Family Collaboration

Family partnerships are relationships that teachers, speech-language pathologists, and other professionals form in order to plan and support Individualized Education Programs (IEPs) or Individualized Family Service Plans (IFSPs) for children with speech or language impairments. Among the specific instructional strategies these collaborations provide are adapting lesson plans, preteaching vocabulary and content, and organizing cooperative learning activities (Turnbull et al., 2007).

One of the most supportive things a parent or other care provider can do for a child with a speech and language delay or disorder is to accept the child and their developmental level and provide language stimulation appropriate to that level. The effectiveness of therapy is enhanced when parents communicate to the child a positive attitude toward the people and activities involved in therapy and when an honest exchange is maintained between parent and therapist. (Dunlap, 2008, p. 151)

Classroom Interventions

Following are several strategies that you will find beneficial in including children with speech or language impairments into the classroom setting. Most importantly, you should seek the assistance of speech-language pathologists because their recommendations for instructions are based on specific assessments targeting the type of speech and/or language impairment the child exhibits. Those children with significant speech and language impairments may benefit from the use of assistive technology devices.

OBSERVATION

Most families and teachers know the importance of observing children's development. Speech or language impairments can be identified as you watch children's interactions with others in the classroom. Your observations are critical in determining whether children should be referred to a speech-language pathologist for a full comprehensive assessment. It is important for you to keep anecdotal information about children's speech and perceived language difficulties to document referrals.

RESPONDING TO STUTTERING AND DISFLUENCY

Several strategies can be put into place within the classroom and home setting to help children with stuttering problems. Some general suggestions are:

- Do not interrupt a child when he is speaking. Allow him to finish his sentence or what he is trying to convey (regardless of how long it takes the child to complete his thought).
- Rephrase any sentences in which the child may have used incorrect grammar or pronunciation (this should be done with a calm tone).
- Do not signal out a child to respond to a question in front of his or her peers or family.
- Model appropriate rate and tone of speech.

◆ Decrease stressful situations and minimize anxiety-producing activities.

SPEECH AND LANGUAGE ASSESSMENTS

Speech and language assessments are important to determine difficulties in children's overall expressive and/or receptive language. Speech-language pathologists are able to define the steps that are necessary to change children's use of language through individualized therapy sessions (Turnbull et al., 2007). As previously mentioned, most speech and language assessments involve the administration of informal and standardized assessments. The specific assessments are designed to measure receptive language skills, expressive language skills, auditory skills, articulation and phonology, pragmatics, oral-motor functioning, voice quality, fluency, and thinking skills. In many cases where the assessment of young children is involved, a team or group approach to assessment is used. The results of the evaluation will be used to develop the IFSP or IEP goals.

TALKING BOOKS

Talking books are digital books prepared by you or family volunteers. They often include photographs of children's friends and family and are developed through programs such as Microsoft PowerPoint, IntelliPics Studio, IntelliTalk, or My Own Bookshelf. These books usually are used with children in the primary grades to motivate them to develop beginning reading skills. However, the interactive design of these books encourages preschool children to "read" a story by looking at the pictures, or listen to the story if sound is added. Like classroom listening centers, these books allow children to hear appropriate language models that they can imitate, and the books can be personalized if computers and appropriate software are available.

ASSISTIVE TECHNOLOGY

The term *augmentative and alternative communication systems* (AAC) refers to the use of a technological device or system in addition to or in lieu of verbal communication. AAC includes gestural systems (e.g., sign language), low-tech visual systems (e.g., eye gaze boards) and high-tech computerized devices (e.g., voice or visual output systems; Dunlap, 2008). AAC systems range from low-tech devices such as picture or letter boards to which the child points to an object to express his desires, to computers with touch screens to assist learners that often are made available to children with speech or language impairments. IDEA (2004) defined these systems as "assistive technology and supplementary aids." Deciding which aid is best for any given child depends on the collaborative team that works with the child. However, cost always seems to be a prohibitive factor, and their purchase may not be within most childcare center budgets.

A simple device that encourages verbal language during play is the Speak Easy Voice Output Communication Aid, which can be ordered from AbleNet (see the company's address at the end of the chapter; Gould & Sullivan, 2005). A Speak Easy is a vocal output communication aide (VOCA), an electrical device that will assist children or adults who are unable to utilize natural speech in communicating their wants and needs. Laptops, handheld devices, and desktop computers all can be used as a VOCA.

Graphic Organizers

Graphic organizers, which are visual representations of stories and curriculum content, are used to help children remember information they learn in their classrooms. The representations may appear on bulletin boards, charts or posters, teacher-made or child-made books, flannel board activities, the chalkboard, or hand-drawn web designs. For example, after reading the book *The Very Hungry Caterpillar*, you might ask the children to draw all of the items the caterpillar ate on a piece of poster board. Hang this in the classroom to serve as a reminder of the story's content. Or you might draw a web on the chalkboard and brainstorm with the children all of the foods the caterpillar ate. Figure 5 provides an example of this.

Pause and Wait

Pause and Wait is a strategy in which teachers or caregivers provide a response time that is longer than that given for a typically developing peer. When a child expects something to occur and it does not, a situation is created where a strong need to communicate occurs. By providing additional time for a response, a child with a speech or language impairment can process the incoming information and organize a response to the posed question (Cook et al., 2008).

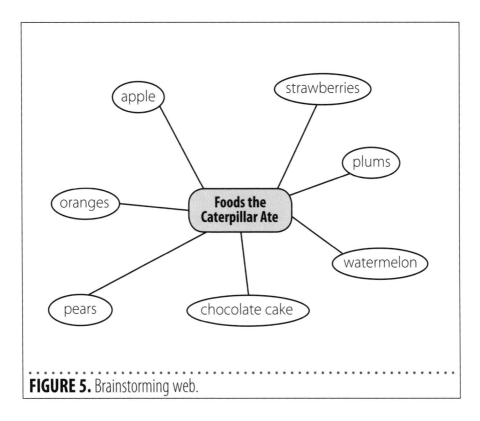

FIGURE 5. Brainstorming web.

Applying the Strategies

Andrew arrived in Mr. Neuwirth's prekindergarten classroom as a child who was almost nonverbal. Mr. Neuwirth realized early in the school year that his approach to speech production would be difficult for him to understand, and throughout the year he struggled to interpret his responses and communication during group work and in individual contact with him.

Mr. Neuwirth immediately began a proactive approach to help Andrew transition into his classroom. Some of the strategies he used also would be helpful for other children who have speech or language impairments.

WORKING WITH THE WHOLE CLASS

When working with the whole class, Andrew's teacher used the following strategies to facilitate communication:

- *Increase interaction between adults and children:* Mr. Neuwirth realized the importance that interaction plays in developing communication skills. He paid special attention to fostering interactive opportunities where communication became functional for Andrew. For example, he responded to what Andrew had to say, listened attentively to him, and expanded on what he had to say. The interactions were those that were functional, or meaningful to Andrew, rather then having Andrew respond to predetermined cues.

- *Teach familiar words*: Teach and use familiar words and language with children and allow children to repeat common words.

- *Introduce new vocabulary*: When introducing new events or skills, Mr. Neuwirth would teach the vocabulary in depth. It was important to Andrew that Mr. Neuwirth focused on using the new words in all contexts so that he was able to generalize the new vocabulary across settings. Mr. Neuwirth also would take time to verbally label objects in their natural setting.

- *Use open-ended questions*: Mr. Neuwirth talked to all of the children in small groups or in Circle Time using open-ended questions so that any child would feel free to answer. For example, instead of asking, "What color is this crayon?" he would say, "What can you tell me about this crayon?"

- *Build on opportunities*: Mr. Neuwirth used all of the opportunities presented to him to implement interventions. For example, when someone lost a shoe at recess (although not planned), Mr. Neuwirth built on this opportunity by stating, "Andy lost his shoe. Look. I see Andy's shoe. I see Andy's blue tennis shoe."

- *Provide CDs of stories*: Mr. Neuwirth encouraged all children, as well as Andrew, to use the classroom Listening Center to listen to CDs of well-known stories and books. In addition, he encouraged Andrew's family to purchase or borrow CDs to use to model language at home.

- *Encourage the child to elaborate*: Whenever possible, Mr. Neuwirth tried to expand all of the children's language by having them elaborate on their words or doing it for them. For example, if Andrew said, "Me baw," he said to him, "Andrew, are you saying you want the ball or that you have the ball?" The teacher could then communicate Andrew's response to his peers, if necessary.

- *Use repetitive language and sounds*: To help all of the children in the class, Mr. Neuwirth taught them familiar rhymes, songs, and fingerplays and repeated them often. Repetition of sounds helps children with language impairments improve their speech production.

WORKING WITH INDIVIDUAL CHILDREN

When working with children with speech and/or language impairments, the teachers should refer to the goals outlined in the child's IFSP or IEP. "Specific language goals should be outlined, and appropriate situations that allow for the development of these should be fostered" (Hooper & Umansky, 2009, p. 331). When working one-on-one with Andrew, his teacher used the following strategies.

- *Model appropriate speech and speech production*: Mr. Neuwirth used every opportunity to model appropriate speech production to children with language impairments. He would match Andrew's words with a more elaborate or appropriate word. He also was cognizant of commenting on Andrew's speech patterns. For example, when Andrew would use a single word for a phrase or request, Mr. Neuwirth would respond to his request and expand on it. In one instance, Andrew said "hat" when he wanted to obtain a baker's hat from the dramatic play center. Mr. Neuwirth repeated and recast what Andrew was requesting and pointing to, stating, "Hat. That is a hat. You want the hat."

- *Consult a speech-language pathologist*: Mr. Neuwirth contacted a speech-language pathologist in the local school district to determine if Andrew could receive speech and hearing screening. He also asked the specialist for literature to help him communicate with children who have speech or language impairments. In addition, Mr. Neuwirth contacted the American Speech-Language-Hearing Association (ASHA) to find resources that would help his work with Andrew. In the public school system, speech-language pathologists often are available on a full- or part-time basis to provide ongoing support to classroom teachers. One suggestion that the speech-language pathologist made was to have Mr. Neuwirth hold up a mirror and ask Andrew to watch his mouth and tongue when he said a word or phrase. Then he asked him to repeat each word while looking into the mirror to find out if his speech production resembled that of his teacher. Mr. Neuwirth demonstrated this technique to Andrew's mother so she could do the same activity at home.

- *Use developmental checklists*: Mr. Neuwirth asked his school administrator (center director) for developmental checklists for assessing language skills to use with children who have suspected problems. The information obtained allowed Mr. Neuwirth to collect information that would be beneficial to the speech-language pathologist in developing specific goals for Andrew.

- *Make an intentional observation schedule*: Mr. Neuwirth began an intentional observation schedule of Andrew's activities and speech production to help him understand the words Andrew was able to appropriately use. Mr. Neuwirth observed Andrew during Center Time for 10 minutes each day. He took notes of the language Andrew used so that he could convey the information to speech professionals. Because his observation allowed him to comprehend Andrew's language production, it helped Mr. Neuwirth to communicate better with Andrew.

- *Listen to Andrew's responses*: Mr. Neuwirth listened attentively to what Andrew had to say. Even when he could not clearly understand what Andrew was articulating he used nonverbal signals (e.g., nodding his head, smiling, looking at Andrew with interest) so that Andrew was aware that what he had to say was important. Mr. Neuwirth assured Andrew frequently that everyone would have opportunities to speak in class.

- *Shorten sentence length*: Mr. Neuwirth soon realized that Andrew had difficulty responding to him when he used long, lengthy sentences. Soon Mr. Neuwirth began to shorter his sentences and avoided complex sentences. He also recast words and phrases. He did increase his sentence length and complexity as Andrew demonstrated improvements in his ability to understand language and communicate more efficiently.

- *Observe the child's peers*: Mr. Neuwirth identified children who knew Andrew and possibly went to preschool with him prior to prekindergarten. He observed their interactions to learn their communication skills. This helped him communicate better with Andrew, because he was becoming more attuned to his language production. Also, he paired these children with Andrew when they went on field trips, had fire drills, or left the room for events or activities so that they could engage in conversation with Andrew about what was going on.

- *Slightly exaggerate intonation patterns*: Mr. Neuwirth slightly exaggerated the key words in his speech. He spoke clearly and paused in between his sentences. He also used an appropriate volume and pace when speaking to Andrew.
- *Use picture cards*: If a child's language production is limited, prepare picture cards for the child to define his needs by pointing to a specific picture. For example, a child may point to the appropriate card when he needs to use the bathroom, choose a center, or indicate that he needs help. One popular form of picture communication is the use of a Picture Exchange Communication System (PECS). When using this method, the child does not directly point to a specific picture. Typically, children are taught to remove a Velcro®-attached picture from a board or binder and hand it to the individual with whom they are communicating. The system is an effective one, and one of the greatest strengths of this system is that social interaction is required.

WORKING WITH FAMILIES

Andrew's teacher used the following strategies when working with his family:

- *Develop a collaborative relationship with families*: Mr. Neuwirth called Andrew's family early in the school year to start developing a collaborative relationship. "Collaboration between professionals and caregivers is always an essential ingredient. The importance of communication in our society demands that its development be a high priority in programs for young children with special needs" (Hooper & Umansky, 2009, p. 337).
- *Encourage families to work with children at home*: Mr. Neuwirth suggested that Andrew's family demonstrate how to make sounds with Andrew at home, sharing the mirror strategy that he used in the classroom for modeling appropriate speech and speech production. Other strategies that were shared with the family included:
  - Use songs at home to transition between activities.
  - Read nightly with your child.
  - Label objects in the home setting.
  - Ask Andrew questions about what is happening at home while it is occurring. For example, ask Andrew what he is doing while he is building with leaves and sticks outside.

- Show enthusiasm when Andrew is successful at tasks.
- Reinforce the use of appropriate language through verbal praise and encouragement.

- *Make activities meaningful and purposeful*: A family must assist in making language development meaningful for the child across multiple settings. If Andrew knows the purposes of listening and communicating, he will have more meaningful experiences.

SAFETY FIRST

For children who have speech or language impairments, the following tips are important (some of these tips may not be appropriate for all children with speech or language impairments):
- As children arrive in the morning or leave to go home, try to talk to them individually to determine if they have anything they want to share with you.
- Whenever you give instructions to the entire group, check to make sure that children with speech or language impairments understand their classroom responsibilities.
- If children are riding home with a parent or guardian, supervise them as they get into the car.
- If they are riding on a bus (or in a van), supervise them as they get into the vehicle.
- Ensure that parents or guardians are aware of when their children are to arrive home or to the bus stop.
- Teach all children about safety drills (e.g., fire or tornado), and work with those who need more help in understanding what they need to know.
- Encourage the use of both verbal and nonverbal safety strategies.

IF YOU WANT TO KNOW MORE

American Speech-Language-Hearing Association (ASHA)
2200 Research Boulevard
Rockville, MD 20850-3289
800-638-8255
http://www.asha.org

Childhood Apraxia of Speech Association of North America (CASANA)
1151 Freeport Road #243
Pittsburgh, PA 15238
412-343-7102
http://www.apraxia-kids.org

Cleft Palate Foundation
1504 East Franklin St., Ste. 102
Chapel Hill, NC 27514-2820
919-933-9044
http://www.cleftline.org

Stuttering Foundation of America
3100 Walnut Grove Road, Ste. 603
Memphis, TN 38111-0749
800-992-9392
http://www.stutteringhelp.org

AbleNet (SpeakEasy Device)
2808 Fairview Avenue North
Roseville, MN 55113
800-322-0956
http://www.ablenetinc.com

Speech Sound Recognition in Young Children
http://www.suite101.com/article.cfm/speech_language_disorders/29689/1

Kiesha

A CHILD WITH A HEARING IMPAIRMENT

As Kiesha and her mother walk toward the preschool Kiesha attends, one of her classmates calls out her name along with a friendly hello. Although the child yells loudly, Kiesha does not turn her head toward the child or respond. Her mother waves at the child and, after a moment of hesitation, Kiesha does the same. As they enter the classroom, Kiesha remains silent and does not look around much. Her teacher, Ms. Able, notices that Kiesha seems focused on where she is going, but does not pay attention to others who stop to talk to her mother or to welcome her.

When Kiesha's teacher approaches her, Kiesha smiles but does not respond verbally. Casey, another child in the class, approaches her and invites her to join him in the Block Center. Once more, Kiesha fails to respond. Ms. Able prompts Kiesha to move toward the center with Casey. Kiesha begins to build a tower with the wooden blocks, and Casey asks her what she is building. She attempts to respond, but her speech is difficult to understand and she becomes frustrated.

Kiesha becomes easily frustrated when others cannot understand her, so when Casey asks her again what she is building, she gives up trying to explain and turns her back to him as she continues to build. As other children arrive, Kiesha does not appear to notice the noise or movement taking place, nor does she seem distracted by the conversations between her teacher and the other children in the classroom.

OVERVIEW OF HEARING IMPAIRMENT

Hearing loss often goes undetected, which means many children with hearing loss do not receive early intervention. It is not unusual for a child's hearing loss to be detected as late as 5 or 6 years of age. You can help families identify early signs of hearing loss by informing them if you notice a child exhibiting any of the following signs:

- speaking too loudly or too quietly,
- using a pitch in speech that is too high or too low,
- not responding to questions appropriately,
- frequently requesting that you repeat directions,
- not replying when called on to answer a question,
- complaining of earaches or ear pain,
- pulling on or tugging at ears,
- frequent ear infections,
- frequent headaches, or
- moving closer to you when you are reading books or talking to small groups.

Signs and symptoms are different for all children. If you notice a child who exhibits one or more of these signs, it is recommended that the child receive a screening for possible hearing loss. Preschool teachers often see these subtle signs that a child might have a problem, but mistake the symptoms of hearing loss as misbehavior or learning difficulties. If you suspect a problem, there also are checklists you can use that indicate developmental progress. These are simple tools you can use to determine whether you should refer a child to an audiologist. Many of these checklists are available online as a tool for families and teachers alike. Once a child's hearing impairment has been detected, it is important to have a general understanding of what a hearing impairment is and how this impairment will affect the child in the classroom.

Professionals often use the term *hearing impairment* to describe hearing loss. There are three types of hearing loss that a child may have: conductive hearing loss, sensorineural hearing loss, and mixed hearing loss. Conductive hearing loss, which is the most common type of hearing loss, usually is treatable through medication or surgery. This type of loss often is a sign of impacted earwax, fluid in the ear, allergies, and/or infection. Sensorineural loss is not treatable by medications or surgery and indicates

Table 5
FIVE MOST COMMON CATEGORIES OF HEARING LOSS

Type of Loss	Definition
Normal range or no impairment (0 dB to 20 dB)	Child detects all speech sounds.
Mild loss (20 dB to 40 dB)	Child may miss up to approximately half of the classroom discussions.
Moderate loss (40 dB to 60 dB)	Child is capable of understanding conversation occurring up to 5 feet away. However, hearing aids and FM systems are necessary to hear sounds occurring farther than 5 feet away.
Severe loss (60 dB to 80 dB)	Child may need full-time amplification to engage actively in all activities within the inclusive classroom. She will need significant help in language and speech development.
Profound loss (80 dB or more)	Child will possibly need a greater degree of intervention in the classroom. Most children with profound loss rely on alternate forms of communication, which may include sign language or the use of a Picture Exchange Communication System.

that the problem lies within the inner ear or nerve passages to the inner ear. This form of hearing loss usually is permanent. Mixed hearing loss occurs when a child has a combination of sensorineural and conductive loss.

There are several assessments available for determining the degree of the child's hearing loss. Most commonly, an audiologist administers an initial audiological assessment. The audiologist is trained in diagnosing, treating, and managing individuals with hearing loss and balance disorders. Typically, a child will receive an audiological assessment upon referral to an audiologist. The audiological assessment measures hearing loss in decibels (dB) across a range of frequencies (Hertz, Hz). For example, a child with a normal range of hearing would experience a range of 0 dB to 20 dB. This assessment will help determine a person's degree of hearing loss. People with hearing impairments may have a partial loss or complete loss of hearing (deaf). In addition, a person with a hearing impairment can experience a loss in one or both ears. Table 5 presents the five most common categories of hearing loss; they are based on the child's degree and severity of loss.

The chart indicates the level of hearing loss, but it is important to remember that:

audiometric descriptions of hearing loss (dB and Hz) do not adequately describe how well a student might be able to use his or her residual (remaining) hearing for learning, especially if amplification is helpful and if the loss does not interfere with hearing human speech. (Taylor, Smiley, & Richards, 2008, p. 257)

As indicated above, the results of the assessment are critical in determining the amount of support a child will need in her classroom setting. For example, a child with significant hearing impairment may need amplification as well as support in both expressive and receptive language, as does a child with moderate hearing loss. However, she also may need support with social development. Often children with significant hearing impairments will face difficulties in making and maintaining friendships. It also is possible that if such an impairment goes undiagnosed or untreated, low self-esteem and behavior problems may occur as a result of limited abilities to communicate effectively.

The American Speech-Language-Hearing Association (ASHA, 2007) identified areas in which a hearing loss can affect children, including:

- It causes delay in the development of receptive and expressive communication skills (speech and language).
- The language deficit causes learning problems that result in reduced academic achievement.
- Communication difficulties often lead to social isolation and poor self-concept.

In addition, ASHA identified five specific areas that hearing loss can affect: vocabulary, sentence structure, speaking, academic achievement, and social functioning.

It is important to know the type of hearing loss a child in your classroom has, as well as the kind of support he will need to be successful in the inclusive setting. Regardless of the degree of hearing loss, new technological advances make it possible for children with hearing impairments to attend inclusive schools successfully with peers who have no hearing impairments.

WHAT TEACHERS NEED TO KNOW ABOUT HEARING IMPAIRMENTS

Teachers often overlook or misidentify children with hearing impairments as having behavioral problems. A child with a hearing impairment might:

- often say "what" or "huh,"
- speak in a loud voice,
- need people to raise their voices so she can hear them,
- inconsistently respond to verbal directions or answer questions that are on his cognitive level,
- not turn his head when his name is called,
- turn her head to whoever is speaking consistently in an effort to see the speaker's face,
- listen to music at a very loud volume,
- have limited use of verbal language,
- appear to ignore the speaker, or
- frequently ask for questions to be repeated.

It is easy to see why a child with a hearing impairment may seem inattentive to your directions. This frequently occurs in children with behavioral concerns. If you suspect a hearing impairment, immediately notify the child's family or center director. The type and degree of the child's hearing loss will directly affect the level of support that he will need in the inclusive setting. Children with a mild loss of hearing often exhibit subtle, easily overlooked signs. However, even a mild loss can directly affect a child's speech and language development. Because hearing loss affects the pitch in which the child hears differently, the high frequency speech sounds (f, s, sh, th) usually are more difficult for a child to produce and hear.

Once identified, it is important to be aware of and report any changes in the child's behavior. To develop an intervention that meets the needs of the child requires the implementation of routine audiological exams as well as ongoing speech and language assessment. However, this information will only benefit the child if paired with observational data you provide. It is important to gather information not only on the child's academic progress, but also on whether or not the child indicates concerns about background noise or his ability to hear classroom discussions. You also can observe the child for answers to common questions such as:

- How often does the child adjust her hearing aid?
- Does the child willingly use her hearing aid?
- Does the child frequently ask others to repeat directions or parts of conversations?
- Does the child consistently lean one side of his face toward the speaker?
- Does the child complain of any discomfort to his ears?
- Are there particular sounds that the child struggles to say?
- Does the child cover her ears when she hears very loud sounds?

HEARING IMPAIRMENT: INCLUSIVE LEARNING STRATEGIES

Like many teachers in today's preschools, you may not have adequate training in disability awareness or inclusive learning. However, many children with hearing impairments attend public and private childcare facilities. In addition to working closely with those trained specifically to work with children with hearing impairments (audiologists and speech-language pathologists) and attending any ongoing professional development in inclusive practices, consider using the following strategies.

Family Interventions

Families with children who have a hearing impairment will find many ways to communicate with their children. Developing various physical and visual cues is beneficial. If the child is using sign language in the preschool setting, it is extremely important that the child continue to use this form of communication at home with her family. Just as there are many different dialects in the spoken language, there also are many forms of sign language. The preferred system within the deaf community is American Sign Language. This is of particular importance to know to assure that the same system is being used across settings.

If a student wears an assistive hearing device such as a hearing aid or has a cochlear implant, it is essential that open lines of communication exist between the teacher, family, and audiologist involved in the child's care to assure the optimal use of the hearing device. It is of great importance that all individuals ensure that the child is wearing the device consistently across settings.

Classroom Interventions

In order for children with special needs to succeed in the classroom, you can make a few of the following accommodations to facilitate their learning process. Be sure to check with the child's family regarding the recommendations made by the child's audiologist. Learn about the child's hearing aid from the audiologist. A hearing aid is not as simple as a pair of glasses and may require adjustments during the school day. Once a child is used to wearing a hearing aid and when it is functioning properly the child usually will want to wear it. Some general suggestions for encouraging a child to wear his or her hearing aid include checking the batteries daily (having a spare set available), keeping the controls on the device set properly (cover the controls so the child can not adjust them manually), keep the ear molds clean and well kept, teach the child to insert and remove his own hearing device (work with the family on this), encourage the family to have a special place at home to store the hearing device, and pay special attention to the acoustic characteristics within the classroom setting and attempt to reduce any extraneous noise (Cook et al., 2008).

Using an FM System

An FM system (available from suppliers of equipment for the hearing impaired) is an amplification system consisting of a receiver and a cordless microphone. This is a group assistive listening device. The child with a hearing impairment wears the receiver around his neck and you speak into a cordless microphone, which allows the child to hear you. You can share the microphone with other children so the child with a hearing impairment can hear them too (make sure to monitor this activity). Usually, children use the FM system in conjunction with a hearing aid.

When the child with a hearing impairment arrives each morning, he puts on the FM system receiver (store it somewhere in the classroom that allows the child easy access to it). You wear the microphone and turn it on when you specifically want the child to hear what you are saying, and then turn the microphone off when you have conversations with other children and colleagues. When classroom noise overwhelms his ability to hear—such as during lunchtime—the child can turn off the receiver, but continue to wear his hearing aid. Only use an FM system if specialists working with the child recommend it.

EMPLOYING PROXIMITY CONTROL

You probably use proximity control occasionally with all the children. This involves simply moving closer to the child so she can hear what you say or signaling to her to move to a specific location in the classroom where she will be able to hear more easily. After group instruction, take the child with a hearing impairment aside and repeat the information.

USING PHYSICAL AND VISUAL CUES

To make sure that the child with a hearing impairment is listening, touch him on the arm or shoulder, stand in front of him, or use some other signal to gain the child's attention. You may want to share these strategies with all of the children so they can get the child's attention. Flashing classroom lights on and off is another way to capture all of the children's attention.

Use picture cards to help the child with a hearing impairment know what she needs to do at various points during the day. Pictures could include:
- a child doing a classroom activity (e.g., putting a puzzle together, building with blocks);
- a line of children to signify line-up time;
- a child eating a snack or helping with snack set-up;
- children sleeping (naptime);
- children on the playground;
- a child putting on her coat, hat, and mittens; and
- children sitting in Circle Time.

You will discover that using actual photographs of the child with a hearing impairment demonstrating the aforementioned classroom behaviors will help her to identify more easily with the task presented. For instance, if you take an actual photograph of the child sleeping during naptime, the child will have a better understanding of the behavioral expectations during naptime. This will provide an opportunity for her to respond positively to your request for the desired behavior.

Learning American Sign Language

If you do not know American Sign Language (ASL), you may want to enroll in a continuing education course in a nearby university or community college to learn some basic signs. There also are several sign language books available at local bookstores. Consider teaching all of the children in the class the alphabet in sign language. Using the signs with the entire class broadens their understanding of what it means to be hearing impaired and it helps foster their communication with the child. (You can purchase American Sign Language charts at your local teacher supply store or go to the Center for Disability Information and Referral [CeDIR] at http://www.Isdd.Indiana.edu/cedir/kidsweb/asl.html.)

Another strategy is to consult with the child's family to learn essential signs (such as "Line up" or "Restroom") that represent words or phrases you often use in the classroom.

Tapping Into Other Senses

During classroom music time, encourage the child with a hearing impairment to sit near the classroom CD player so she can feel the vibrations of the music. By "feeling" the pulsations of the music, she can participate in the musical activity as her peers are singing, moving, or dancing. Consider providing a headset for children with hearing impairments so that you can turn up the music loudly without hurting other children's ears. However, use caution in determining the "loudness" of the music. In addition, if the children are using musical instruments, select those instruments that produce sounds falling within the range of the child's ability to hear. For example, some children may not be able to hear a flute as well as they can hear cymbals or drums.

Using a Peer Buddy

A peer buddy is another child in the classroom who helps guide the child with a hearing impairment through the day's activities. For example, when children are on the playground, the child with a hearing impairment may not hear the whistle blow to signal that it is time to go inside. The peer buddy makes sure that the child with a hearing impairment follows the rest of the group inside, perhaps with a visual cue or signal of some sort or by taking her by the hand and leading her inside. Other times when having a peer buddy is appropriate are:

- lining up to go home or to another part of the building,
- locating a table and chair for lunch,
- leading the child to a center for activities,
- demonstrating how to do a special art project (because the child might not have heard all of the directions), and
- encouraging the child to become an active participant in all classroom experiences.

Applying the Strategies

When Kiesha's teacher approaches her, Kiesha smiles but does not respond verbally. Casey, another child in the class, approaches her and invites her to join him in the Block Center. Once more, Kiesha fails to respond. Ms. Able prompts Kiesha to move toward the center with Casey. Kiesha begins to build a tower with the wooden blocks, and Casey asks her what she is building. She attempts to respond, but her speech is difficult to understand and she becomes easily frustrated.

If you are fortunate enough to know ahead of time that a child with a specific disability will be joining your classroom, you can take a proactive approach in preparing for the child's arrival. Ms. Able began immediately to prepare the environment when she learned that Kiesha would be in her classroom.

WORKING WITH THE WHOLE CLASS

When a child with a hearing impairment is included in the inclusive setting, accommodations that focus on visual aspects of communication are advantageous. Some of the strategies Kiesha's teacher used include:

- *Use photographs as visual aids*: Ms. Able took photographs of Kiesha to demonstrate activities. She prepared a poster so Kiesha and her peers would know the schedule of the day and would recognize when activities would be changing.
- *Include technology in classroom instruction*: A wide variety of technological advances can be used to enhance instruction. For example, some of the teachers of older children may use closed-captioned versions of videos.
- *Incorporate sign language into the class*: Integrate sign language into the daily schedule. All children will benefit from learning and

using simple signs. Use signs that indicate transitions, speaking quietly or louder, and so on. The most important signs to use are those that are considered to be frequently occurring words. A good resource for learning sign language is *Simple Signing With Young Children: A Guide for Infant, Toddler, and Preschool Teachers* by Carol Garboden Murray (2007). Ms. Able asked her administrator to order a few additional copies of the book so parents wanting to teach their children sign language would have the same resource book. The Handspeak Web site (http://www. handspeak.com) also was helpful to Kiesha's teacher.

- *Use concrete objects during daily lessons*: Utilize puppets, pictures, stuffed animals, and other concrete objects when conducting classroom activities. Pairing concrete objects with songs, rhymes, and books will enable a child with a hearing impairment to follow along better with the classroom activity.

- *Use nonverbal communication to support speech*: Facial expressions and gestures can be paired with speech and are essential in communicating with visual language. Facial expressions can help to clarify the tone of the conversation. Very young children may need to have signs and facial expressions exaggerated or repeated (often referred to as child-directed signing).

- *Increase role-playing activities*: Preschool children with hearing impairments can benefit from role-playing as a means to increase story comprehension. The role-playing activity will reinforce the vocabulary and storyline of the narrative.

- *Correct tone:* Remind all children of the correct tone and volume of speech. If a child is speaking too loudly or softly, bring it to his attention and model the appropriate tone and volume.

WORKING WITH INDIVIDUAL CHILDREN

In working one-on-one with Kiesha, her teacher employed the following strategies:

- *Minimize background noise*: Children with hearing aids or cochlear implants often have difficulty with amplification of random classroom sounds, such as air conditioners, movement of chairs and tables, and filters from aquariums. Minimize background noises by placing small fabric pads under chair and table legs. Use carpet pieces in specific areas of the classroom and, if possible, avoid having noisy classroom pets such as fish tanks and hamsters (the trails and wheels are noisy). Carpeting throughout the room is beneficial, if it is possible. (*Note*: Keep in mind that even with good amplification, hearing aids will cause sound distortions for children.) Ms. Able also received training in the care and handling of Kiesha's hearing aids.

- *Use visual cues*: Use a visual cue to capture the child's attention. This visual cue can be as simple as a hand wave, but other gestures might include touching your nose, pulling on your ear, or other motions that you have explained to the child. Ms. Able and Kiesha agreed on a cue that Kiesha could use when she needed help or needed to have directions repeated.

- *Increase the use of concrete objects during instruction*: Most children enjoy the use of flannel board pieces or puppets during story time. A child with a hearing impairment, like Kiesha, highly benefits from the enhanced comprehension opportunities and vocabulary development that occurs when props and puppets are used to illustrate actions occurring in the story.

- *Face the child when speaking*: Ms. Able faced Kiesha directly when giving directions or speaking to her. Many children with hearing impairments, including preschoolers, rely on reading lips to clarify the information being presented. Ms. Able kept her hands away from her face so Kiesha could interpret her facial expressions and see her lips as she spoke. It is important to keep your lip movements as normal as possible, not yelling or speaking loudly, because the child needs to learn to "read" normal speech.

- *Seat the child to maximize her understanding*: During Circle Time, Ms. Able placed Kiesha close to the front of the group during her most direct instruction. If possible, arrange the children in a semicircle and seat the child with a hearing impairment at the center of the arch, allowing her to see your face while you speak. You might want to create an "open movement policy" ahead of time. This policy would allow the child to relocate herself to hear discussions more clearly.

- *Check for the child's understanding*: After giving directions or explaining a task, Ms. Able would check for understanding by asking Kiesha to repeat or paraphrase the directions she had given.

- *Identify the student and peers by name*: Although this seems like a simple strategy, it proved beneficial to Kiesha. When Ms. Able identified students in the class by name before speaking to them, it allowed Kiesha the opportunity to identify the person to whom the conversation was directed.
- *Eliminate excessive words:* Mrs. Able was careful not to use an abundance of unnecessary words to describe an activity. Kiesha would become overwhelmed when too much verbal information was presented to her.

Working With Families

Kiesha's teacher used the following strategies when working with Kiesha's family:

- *Learn from children's families*: Ms. Able talked to Kiesha's family so that she could learn what procedures they used at home to communicate with Kiesha (i.e., American Sign Language, physical and visual cues). Ms. Able wanted to incorporate the strategies used at home when working with Kiesha in the classroom. She talked to Kiesha's peers about the strategies they could use to communicate with their classmate and taught them some simple signs. One of the strategies that Kiesha's parents use at home is using pointing to direct Kiesha's attention while still permitting language input.
- *Use videotaped documentation*: Many teachers have found success in using a videotaped session to document the communication behaviors of a child during the school day. This tape can be shared with the family so they can assist you and help to develop responsive communicative behaviors with their child (Raver, 2009).
- *Open doors for building friendships*: Provide opportunities for families to meet with other families in your school who have hearing-impaired children. This particularly is beneficial if you know other children in the school who are hearing impaired who are older than the child in your classroom.
- *Encourage parents to create daily listening games*: Children with hearing impairments should be encouraged to listen for sounds and identify them throughout the day. For example, at home, a child

might listen to the sounds of the dogs barking or dishwasher running.

SAFETY FIRST

Safety for all children is a high priority in any classroom. For children with hearing impairments, the following tips are important:

- As children leave to go home, place children with hearing impairments at the front of the class line so that they can communicate quickly, if necessary.
- If children are riding home with a family member, supervise them as they get into the car.
- If they are riding on a bus or in a van, supervise them as they get into the vehicle. A family member should be waiting at the nearest bus stop to help the child off the bus.
- Teach children about safety drills (e.g., fire or tornado). Have posters available to show children what they need to do in case emergencies arise in the classroom. Use the posters when the entire class is having safety drills in order to prepare the child with hearing impairment for future drills.
- If the signal for the safety drill is one that makes a sound (such as a bell or buzzer) find out if it is possible to install a flashing light that signals at the same time as the bell or buzzer rings. If not, provide a visual cue for the child to respond to that signifies that a safety drill is happening (e.g., a hand motion for fire drill).

When focusing on safety, it is important to teach a child with a hearing impairment "to distinguish various noises, especially what is a background noise compared to a sound that should be the focus of attention" (Raver, 2009, p. 297).

IF YOU WANT TO KNOW MORE

American Speech-Language-Hearing Association (ASHA)
2200 Research Boulevard
Rockville, MD 20850-3289
800-638-8255
http://www.asha.org

Beginnings for Parents of Hearing Impaired Children, Inc.
P.O. Box 17646
Raleigh, NC 27619
919-850-2746
http://www.ncbegin.org

Hearing Loss Association of America
7910 Woodmont Avenue, Ste. 1200
Bethesda, MD 20814
301-657-2248
http://www.hearingloss.org

National Institute on Deafness and Other Communication Disorders
National Institute of Health
31 Center Drive, MSC 2320
Bethesda, MD 20892-2320
301-496-7243
http://nidcd.nih.gov

CHAPTER 7

José

A CHILD WITH AN ORTHOPEDIC IMPAIRMENT

When Ms. Parker's center director asked if she would mind having a child who used a wheelchair in her room, she replied, "No, I don't mind, but I may need some classroom help because I have never had a child in a wheelchair in my class before and I am not sure how much additional assistance he may need." By law, the center director was aware that their center could not turn away any child, but she wanted to be sure that Ms. Parker would be willing to have a child with special needs in her room. The director also wanted to find out if Ms. Parker had any concerns. Ms. Parker, who knew very little about children with disabilities, wanted to know if she would have help in the classroom for José. She asked her director if the school district would provide anyone to help them with José. When her director said yes, Ms. Parker was more comfortable with her ability to help José adjust to the classroom.

Ms. Parker soon learned that José had spina bifida, a condition that affects control of the lower body. José needed to use a wheelchair to help him get around, and because of his impairment, he would need frequent restroom breaks throughout the day. The paraeducator (instructional aide) who would be working with him was trained to help him with his specialized toileting needs. Ms. Parker also arranged classroom materials so they would be easily accessible to José. She planned to include the paraeducator in the lesson planning process.

Her preparation for José's arrival included talking to the children in her classroom about José. She felt that this opportunity to help the children get to know José would be important for developing a relationship with him. If the children welcomed José into their class, then the children would adopt attitudes that would affect their attitudes toward accepting differences in others as they grew older.

OVERVIEW OF ORTHOPEDIC IMPAIRMENTS

An orthopedic impairment (sometimes called a motor impairment) refers to a varied group of conditions with a wide variety of causes. Most frequently, an orthopedic impairment involves the skeletal system (i.e., bones, joints, limbs) and those muscles associated with it. The Individuals with Disabilities Education Improvement Act (IDEA, 2004) defines orthopedic impairment as

> a severe orthopedic impairment that adversely affects a child's educational performance. The term includes impairments caused by congenital anomaly (clubfoot, absence of some member), impairments caused by disease (poliomyelitis, bone tuberculosis), and impairments from other causes (cerebral palsy, amputations, and fractures or burns that cause contractures). (§ 300.A.300.8c8)

Most teachers who have children in their classrooms with orthopedic impairments will likely encounter those children with muscular dystrophy, cerebral palsy, or spina bifida. Each of these conditions has its own set of causes and prevalence and will be examined separately.

Cerebral palsy is a common physical disability occurring in about 1.5 of 1,000 births. It is a lifetime disorder that affects movement ("cerebral" refers to the brain, and "palsy" refers to lack of muscle control). A child has cerebral palsy because his brain cannot control his muscles. There are three primary causes of cerebral palsy: prenatal (infection or malformation of the brain before birth), perinatal (lack of oxygen or infection during birth), or postnatal (brain injury or meningitis after birth).

Many times, children with cerebral palsy or other orthopedic impairments may have one or more limbs that are affected. A child who has quadriplegia will have four extremities affected, whereas a child with two extremities affected on the same side of his body is identified as having hemiplegia. A child with quadriplegia will probably experience more difficulty manipulating the physical environment than a child with one limb affected (monoplegia). How each child learns to compensate for her specific disability will affect that child's actual ability level. Coping skills play a major role in the success levels of children with orthopedic impairments. Children with cerebral palsy may experience other specific limitations including speech problems, hearing loss, vision problems, or seizures.

Regardless of how the child acquires cerebral palsy, the type and degree of the impairment will determine the adaptations and/or modifications that are necessary for the child to participate successfully in the classroom setting. Depending on the degree and severity of the condition, you should be fully aware that collaborating with a team of specialists, including physical therapists and occupational therapists, is essential for the child's success in the classroom.

The second orthopedic impairment that children in the classroom may have is spina bifida, which occurs when the spinal cord does not form properly during fetal development. The higher up on the spinal cord that the impairment occurs, the more severely the person is impaired. Fortunately, medical advances have led to a decrease in the number of individuals born with spina bifida (occurring in one of about every 2,000 births).

Muscular dystrophy is another common orthopedic impairment. There are varying forms of muscular dystrophy, but all indicate a progressive weakening of the muscles. This means that the impairment may develop in the preschool years (such as Duchenne muscular dystrophy, the most prevalent form of muscular dystrophy) and then progressively become worse. For example, a child developing Duchenne muscular dystrophy in preschool may have symptoms of weakness in the lower legs. Soon the muscles weaken in an upward progression in the body and by 8–10 years old, the child may need a wheelchair. This particular form of muscular dystrophy often results in death by age 20. At present, there is no cure or treatment to prevent the further progression of muscular dystrophy.

In addition to the above-mentioned forms of orthopedic impairments, amputations and fractures also are classified as orthopedic impairments. In addition, impairments caused by disease, such as poliomyelitis and bone tuberculosis, are identified as orthopedic impairments. Each of these specific conditions requires special care on the part of the teacher.

WHAT TEACHERS NEED TO KNOW ABOUT ORTHOPEDIC IMPAIRMENTS

Your role will vary depending on the severity and degree of the child's orthopedic impairment. A child with minimal or short-term limitations will need less support in the classroom than a child whose more severe impairment directly affects his ability to function actively as a member of the classroom.

Caregivers often focus on supporting children with orthopedic impairments on a physical level. However, children with orthopedic impairments may find themselves dealing not only with physical limitations, but also potential psychological and emotional implications. The physical limitations imposed on the child often have an indirect impact on the level of social interactions that all children need.

For example, if a child is limited in her ability to run and the other children are engaged in a game of tag outdoors, it is likely that the child will feel isolated from participation. In this instance, continual isolation may lead to her emotional withdrawal. With limited social interactions, the child may find it more difficult to create or maintain friendships.

> The foundation for many games and sports related activities for young children is the development of gross motor skills. Children who have difficulty executing gross motor skills smoothly and efficiently are often frustrated by motor games and may shy away from participation. (Long, Thomas, & Hall, as cited in Raver, 2009, p. 188)

Not all children with orthopedic impairments will experience negatively impacted social and emotional interactions. However, you should be aware that this possibility exists and that appropriate interventions can improve contact with nondisabled peers.

Children with orthopedic impairments may utilize technology to assist them in everyday functioning. Over the last decade, researchers and specialists have introduced a plethora of assistive technology to children with special needs. The Assistive Technology Act of 1998 defined assistive technology as "any item, piece of equipment, or product system, whether acquired commercially, modified, or customized, that is used to increase, maintain, or improve functional capabilities of individuals with disabilities" (S.2432§ 3.a.3). Simply stated, assistive technology is any device or software that can maximize a person's potential or increase that person's abilities to acquire skills.

The use of assistive technology can help a child in the classroom achieve greater independence and rely less frequently on help from you or the child's peers. Using technology can help a child communicate, acquire, and maintain self-help skills and enjoy recreational activities with her same-age peers. For example, special switches are now available to adapt everyday toys so that children with physical limitations can use them.

You will need to familiarize yourself not only with the child's IEP or IFSP, but also with the specific adaptive equipment that a child uses. Occasionally, the child does not need to use special equipment. Often, it is possible to modify everyday toys and materials to increase a child's level of participation in the classroom. Chapter 11 contains more in-depth information on how to adapt and modify toys to meet the needs of all learners in the classroom.

A common misconception is that all children with orthopedic impairments have cognitive impairments. The type and severity of the child's impairment, as well as the duration (how long the child has had the impairment), all will factor into his level of cognitive functioning. Many children with orthopedic impairment have no deficits in cognitive abilities. Understanding a child's specific impairment, including keeping open lines of communication with families and therapists, will help you determine how to interact with and plan for the child.

ORTHOPEDIC IMPAIRMENTS: INCLUSIVE CLASSROOM STRATEGIES

Family Interventions

As soon as a qualified professional identifies a child with orthopedic impairments, family interventions begin. Often, medical professionals work directly with families to assist them with their child's special needs.

Frequently, siblings of a child with an orthopedic impairment may need special support. For instance, if a sibling sees his or her sister having a seizure, that child may become frightened and withdraw. Specially trained counselors and therapists are available to assist families with coping with the emotional stressors of having a child with special needs in the family.

COLLABORATING WITH SPECIAL EDUCATION AND RELATED SERVICES PROFESSIONALS

Because IDEA 2004 requires public school systems to work with families whose young children have disabilities and are soon to enter preschool programs, you can reasonably expect that children with orthopedic impairments have had physical and neurological examinations by medical personnel. Consequently, children should have IEPs, IFSPs, and possibly healthcare plans, all of which define the type of early intervention services the child should receive in his home and childcare center.

MAKING SURE THE CHILD RECEIVES PHYSICAL AND NEUROLOGICAL EXAMINATIONS

Children with orthopedic impairments frequently require medical attention, often as soon as they are born. Occasionally, prenatal screening identifies some physical disabilities. Physical and neurological examinations are the first step in determining a child's muscle strength and endurance, muscle and joint flexibility, mobility, and the extent of any impairment (Turnbull et al., 2007). These examinations are critical when partnering with special education and related services professionals to develop IEPs, IFSPs, and healthcare plans.

HAVING A HEALTHCARE PLAN FOR A CHILD'S SPECIAL MEDICAL NEEDS

Healthcare plans are developed for children who have special medical needs such as a child with cerebral palsy, amputations, fractures, and other congenital anomalies. These plans include procedures for classroom administration of medications, the child's participation in classroom activities, emergency procedures, listings of emergency phone numbers, descriptions of therapy sessions the child may require (e.g., physical or respiratory therapy), and consent forms signed by the child's doctors and parents or guardians. Special education and related services professionals define these plans along with the child's parents or guardians (Turnbull et al., 2007).

Classroom Interventions

As the child's teacher, you have an important role in the professional plan to help families with children who have orthopedic impairments. There are several possible interventions you can implement in the classroom to assist the child in being successful in the inclusive setting. Descriptions of these interventions are below.

Developing Individualized Education Programs (IEP)/Individual Family Service Plans (IFSP)

IEP's and ISFP's specify children's learning goals and outline the services they need. Instructional objectives include both short- and long-term goals (Mastropieri & Scruggs, 2004). A special education and related services team develops the IEP/IFSP with the child's family. In public schools, this team includes the child's teacher. For many children with orthopedic impairments, physical therapy, occupational therapy, and/or speech therapy are addressed in the IEP/IFSP. In addition, assistive technology needs may be addressed in these plans.

Providing Assistive Technology

When using specialized technology with children with special needs, the equipment or devices are referred to as assistive technology (AT). The goal of providing such technology is to encourage independence in children, regardless of their level of impairment. Two basic types of assistive technology are low-tech and high-tech technology. Low-tech devices usually are simple, inexpensive, and often homemade. Examples of low-tech technology include pencil grips, large paper clips used to help children turn pages (if they have small motor problems), and simple switches that allow children to activate classroom toys (Warner & Sower, 2005).

High-tech devices are commercially produced, often more expensive, and include a wide variety of equipment from Braille note takers, power wheelchairs (for children with orthopedic impairments or multiple disabilities), FM systems, and software programs. Computers with high-tech devices are those with voice-activated word processors, screen magnifiers, and alternative keyboards (Warner & Sower, 2005). Because both Part C and Part B of IDEA (2004) addressed AT, AT must be considered and discussed during the IEP/IFSP meeting. This evaluation for AT services should be repeated frequently, as the needs of the child may change over time.

Adapting Physical Education to Fit the Child's Needs

Children with orthopedic impairments have unique physical needs, and their need for physical activity is just as important as it is among their typically developing peers. Related services professionals who address the needs of children with orthopedic impairments can determine their cardiovascular function, muscle strength and endurance, joint flexibility, posture, and mobility (Turnbull et al., 2007). Adaptive physical education instructors receive special training to plan and implement physical education instruction for children with disabilities. If an adaptive physical education instructor is available, consult with him or her. In addition, utilize his or her recommendations and adapt physical activities for each child with an orthopedic impairment.

Developing Positive Self-Esteem

One of the issues that children with orthopedic impairments face is their self-awareness and acceptance of their disability. As children grow older, they may develop low self-esteem because of peer isolation, so your assistance in helping children learn self-acceptance becomes critical. In other words, children with orthopedic impairments have psychological and emotional needs that may be just as important as their physical needs. You will need to work with children's families to help the child acquire self-knowledge and self-acceptance. Wehmeyer, Sands, Knowlton, and Kozleski (2002) recommended that children learn how to:

- identify their own positive characteristics,
- express confidence in themselves,
- interact with others,
- talk about themselves in positive ways,
- accept praise and criticism from others, and
- control their emotions.

Helping children with orthopedic impairments develop these skills will be a challenging task for you and the families of these children, but a concerted effort to help the child in this area will reap positive benefits.

Applying the Strategies

Ms. Parker soon learned that José had spina bifida, a condition that affects control of the lower body. José needed to use a wheelchair to help him get around, and because of his impairment, he would need frequent restroom breaks throughout the day. The paraeducator (instructional aide) who would be working with him was trained to assist him with his specialized toileting needs. Ms. Parker also arranged the classroom materials so they would be easily accessible to José. She planned to include the paraeducator in the lesson planning process.

The strategies described below are based on one teacher's desire to accommodate a child with spina bifida into her classroom. Because orthopedic impairments vary in nature, you will want to learn as much as possible about the specific impairment a child has so you can address it and act accordingly.

WORKING WITH THE WHOLE CLASS

José's teacher used the following methods when working with her entire classroom:

- *Check the classroom environment for accessibility*: Ms. Parker scanned the classroom to determine if any of the centers needed to have wider spaces so José could enter with his wheelchair. She also made sure that José would be able to reach his classroom cubby and his coat hook in the cloakroom (Gould & Sullivan, 2005). Ms. Parker found that the design of many areas of her classroom made it difficult for José to access them. She rearranged the furniture in the room so that José could easily move in his wheelchair from one area to another. The orientation and mobility specialist working with Jose worked closely with Ms. Parker in adapting the physical environment.
- *Plan for bathroom use*: Make plans for bathroom use, especially if children need to leave the classroom to take care of their needs. Ms. Parker was fortunate that she had bathrooms for both genders in her classroom, so she set up a traffic sign configuration to help children when they needed to go to the bathroom. If the sign showed green, then any child could enter. When they needed to use the bathroom, they needed to turn the sign over to red to indicate that the bathroom was in use.

- *Arrange modified movement activities*: Creative movement and games should be planned so that all children can participate and activities are beneficial to everyone. "Play-oriented activities increase the pleasure, engagement, and motivation of a child, the child's parent, and professionals" (Long et al., as cited in Raver, 2009, p. 188).

- *Rearrange items on shelves*: Ms. Parker soon realized that some of the items placed on shelves were too high for José to reach from his wheelchair. She quickly removed those items and placed them at a level where he could easily reach them. This enabled José to reach art supplies and puzzles without being dependent on a peer to get them for him.

- *Use a moveable board instead of a bulletin board*: Ms. Parker often checked the daily weather and attached pictures of weather symbols using Velcro® pieces to a classroom bulletin board. When she learned that José was joining the classroom, she removed the bulletin board and developed a weather chart on a moveable board to help José participate in the daily classroom discussion on the weather (Gould & Sullivan, 2005). When it was José's turn to attach something to the chart, she moved the board to him so he could easily add the new piece.

- *Promote adaptive skills*: Young children, even those with orthopedic impairments, will need to develop self-help or self-care skills. Deficits in gross or fine motor abilities may present several challenges in this area. Adapting the tasks or the environment may assist the child in overcoming the challenges. Ms. Parker was patient with José when he attempted some of these more challenging tasks. Ms. Parker realized that even though she could do some skills such as zipping his pants for José to save time, José needed the opportunity to acquire these skills himself. Raver (2009) identified some specific suggestions to assist with dressing and feeding skills in children with orthopedic impairments:
  - Allow the child time to perform a skill (be patient).
  - Reduce the use of fasteners (e.g., replace zippered pants with elastic pants).
  - When using fasteners, encourage parents to send the child to school using easy to manipulate fasteners such as Velcro® or large buttons.

- Position the child appropriately before having him attempt a dressing skill (e.g., the child may need to sit to dress).
- Consider using slip-on shoes to assist students with fine motor deficits.
- Prior to snack or lunchtime, position the child so that proper trunk (torso) alignment is achieved. If feeding is difficult for a child, reduce distractions so the child can focus on self-feeding.
- Acquire proper adaptive feeding utensils that help to increase independence during feeding.

WORKING WITH INDIVIDUAL CHILDREN

When working one-on-one with José, his teacher implemented the following:

- *Familiarize yourself with the child's IEP/IFSP and healthcare plan:* As soon as Ms. Parker learned that José would be joining the class, she asked if José had an IEP and a healthcare plan. She wanted to familiarize herself with the recommendations in both plans to facilitate his ability to learn in her classroom.

- *Seat children at the same level when possible*: Because it is important for children in wheelchairs to be seated at the same level as the rest of the children, especially during Circle Time (Gould & Sullivan, 2005), Ms. Parker asked her administrator for more chairs for her classroom to accommodate José's needs. For art experiences and fine motor activities (e.g., putting puzzles together, playing with attribute blocks), Ms. Parker asked her center director to purchase a table that a wheelchair could fit under easily. The table also was useful when José had snack or lunch. Because he was able to sit on the floor for short periods, Ms. Parker helped José get out of his wheelchair for centers whenever possible. (The physical therapist helped Ms. Parker learn the proper way to help José in and out of his wheelchair.)

- *Be prepared to help the child with bathroom needs*: Because José had spina bifida, a prenatal condition that causes the spinal cord to form improperly, Ms. Parker knew that he most likely would experience incontinence and problems with bowel movements, and she wanted to be prepared to help him as much as possible.

She researched the condition and read what she could about spina bifida in order to accommodate his needs. This helped Ms. Parker to implement different strategies in her classroom, because she or the classroom aide would have to assist José when he needed to go to the bathroom. In many early childhood classrooms, stepstools often are provided. If a child has poor balance, he many need to have some type of arm supports added to increase his success of independent toileting.

- *Facilitate the child's Block Center play:* Ms. Parker asked other children in the classroom to help José when he wanted to play in the Block Center. For example, they might begin block structures against the wall, and José could add blocks when the structure was tall enough. Another idea for the Block Center is to place building materials, such as Legos® and Lincoln Logs®, on José's wheelchair tray or on top of a small table (Gould & Sullivan, 2005).

- *Plan appropriate gross motor activities*: Ms. Parker searched for gross motor activities that José might be able to participate in during outdoor play. She and his aide developed a Wheelchair Obstacle Course on the playground so he could maneuver his chair around plastic pylons and other playground equipment. José's aide often tossed balls to him so he could practice throwing and catching. Ms. Parker and José's aide also positioned targets near his wheelchair so he could throw balls toward them. They planned activities that José could do out of his wheelchair. For example, Ms. Parker removed him from his wheelchair and seated him in a regular chair for activities in the Puzzle and Manipulatives Center.

- *Teach the child self-care skills*: José's aide developed plans for helping him with his bathroom needs and began teaching him self-care skills that would become necessary for him as he grew older. Ms. Parker learned that she should never push children in wheelchairs unless they ask for assistance (see http://www.as.wvu.edu/~scidis/motor.html for more information).

- *Talk to the child about wheelchair safety*: Ms. Parker also made sure that José knew that the horn on his electric wheelchair was an important safety feature. She explained to him that he needed to alert other children behind him with the horn when he was going to back up (Gould & Sullivan, 2005).

- *Include the child as much as possible in movement activities*: When presenting movement activities in the classroom, Ms. Parker encouraged José to imitate the movements of his peers, even though he was in a wheelchair. Another idea Ms. Parker used was letting José be the timekeeper or "music director" during movement and music activities. José was encouraged to participate in all activities to the extent in which he felt comfortable and at the level at which he could be successful.

- *Learn ways to build the child's self-esteem*: Ms. Parker enrolled in a workshop on building children's self-esteem and looked for additional workshops that addressed the social-emotional needs of children with special needs.

- *Learn how to properly lift the student*: Children with significant motor deficits may need assistance in moving from one location to another. If this is the case, the teacher needs to familiarize herself with proper lifting and carrying techniques. "When a young child is lifted correctly, abnormal reflexes are not stimulated, and the child appears more normal and actually is under less stress" (Cook et al., 2008, p. 237). Teachers should never attempt to move a child with a significant motor impairment without the proper training from a physical therapist, occupational therapist, or adaptive physical educator.

WORKING WITH FAMILIES

Ms. Parker's conferences with José's family focused on how they were helping him learn wheelchair safety, self-help skills, how to participate in movement activities, and tips for building his self-esteem. The family members were able to assist Ms. Parker in understanding the specific needs that José had at home and the procedure that the family was following to support these needs. For instance, José required special assistance at home when interacting with his older sibling. Knowing this information, Ms. Parker was able to create opportunities for these same social skills to be embedded into his classroom activities.

SAFETY FIRST

The following tips are critical to ensure the safety of children with physical or orthopedic impairments:

- Be prepared when out-of-the-ordinary events are planned for the day (e.g., a field trip, a special guest coming in, someone bringing in an animal). Children who use wheelchairs may need assistance to get in and out of buses when wheelchair lifts are unavailable. If planning a field trip, check ahead of time if ramps are available for easy access by children in wheelchairs.

- Children with physical disabilities and orthopedic impairments may need wheelchair lifts on the buses or vans they use for arrival and departure from schools or childcare centers. Children attending public school typically receive transportation to and from school and these vehicles usually are properly equipped. The physical environment should be evaluated to assure that unnecessary barriers are removed that could cause a child with physical limitations to struggle to move around.

- Talk to your administrator about arranging parking spaces near the building for parents if they bring their child to school and pick the child up at the end of the day. Handicapped parking should be available. Requirements for childcare facilities are addressed in ADA.

- Teach children about safety drills (e.g., fire or tornado). Most children with physical or orthopedic impairments will be able to follow emergency procedures. Teachers should ensure that children in wheelchairs, using walkers, or having other physical limitations have someone who is responsible for assisting them when responding to drills or actual emergencies and follow preset plans organized by their schools or childcare centers. Children in wheelchairs and walkers may be required to exit their classrooms or schools by following alternate routes.

IF YOU WANT TO KNOW MORE

National Association of Parents With Children in Special Education
1431 W. South Fork Dr.
Phoenix, AZ 85045
800-754-4421
http://www.napcse.org

TASH
1025 Vermont Ave., NW, Ste. 300
Washington, DC 20005
202-540-9020
http://www.tash.org

National Dissemination Center for Children with Disabilities
1825 Connecticut Ave. NW, Ste. 700
Washington, DC 20009
800-695-0285
http://www.nichcy.org

United Cerebral Palsy
1660 L St., NW, Ste. 700
Washington, DC 20036-5603
800-872-5827
http://www.ucp.org

Muscular Dystrophy Association
3300 E. Sunrise Drive
Tucson, AZ 85718
800-572-1717
http://www.mda.org

Strategies for Teaching Students With Motor/Orthopedic Impairments
http://www.as.wvu.edu/~scidis/motor.html

CHAPTER

8

Emily

A CHILD WITH A VISUAL IMPAIRMENT

Emily, a child in Mrs. Johnson's preschool class, appeared to be a typically developing 3-year-old. Her family had not indicated that Emily might have an identified visual impairment. However, as the year progressed, Mrs. Johnson began to notice Emily display some significant behaviors that could possibly indicate a problem. For example, she noticed that Emily always moved close to her when she showed materials and objects that the children would use in small groups. At first, Mrs. Johnson thought that Emily was probably just a curious child.

Mrs. Johnson became more concerned, though, when she noticed that Emily touched every object that she presented to the class and placed the objects close to her eyes to get a better look. Emily appeared to need the tactile information to comprehend more clearly what the material was and how it related to the classroom learning experience.

Emily also was a bit clumsy when she walked around the classroom. She bumped into classroom furniture regularly and tripped over toys other children were using. Mrs. Johnson noticed that Emily often squinted outdoors because the sun apparently hurt her eyes and prevented her from seeing adequately.

Mrs. Johnson knew she should talk to Emily's family about her concern because if Emily did have vision problems, it would affect her ability to learn.

OVERVIEW OF VISUAL IMPAIRMENTS

Several different definitions and descriptors for visual impairments exist, including a legal definition and the definition found within IDEA (2004). For the purpose of this chapter, the term *visual impairment* means "vision that, even with correction, adversely affects a child's educational performance. The term includes both partial sight and blindness" (IDEA, 2004, Section 300.8 [c] [13]). Educational facilities use this definition to determine a child's eligibility within the public school system.

Legal blindness is not the same as *total blindness*. Determining total blindness requires the consideration of several different characteristics. This is important to note because many legally blind children are still able to read printed materials with assistive technology devices or enlargement of print. In 2005, 54,637 children from birth through age 21 across the country were identified as being legally blind (American Printing House for the Blind [APH], 2005).

The National Dissemination Center for Children with Disabilities (2004) identified terms associated with visual impairments within the context of the educational system. These terms are available below:

- *Partially sighted*: Children with visual problems who require special education services.
- *Low vision*: Children with severe visual impairments. These individuals have sight, but are unable to read at a normal viewing distance, even with the aid of corrective lenses. These children often need adaptations in lighting or size of print in reading material, and rely on other senses for learning. Occasionally, they need Braille texts.
- *Legally blind*: People who have less than 20/200 vision in one stronger eye and/or possess a limited field of vision.
- *Totally blind*: Children who learn via Braille.

Although these definitions will help you to understand some of the needs a child with a visual impairment may have, it is important to understand how the child is best able to use the vision she does have. The use of her vision and the extent of the impairment will depend a great deal on the child's age at the onset of visual impairment, the way the impairment occurred, and which part of the child's eye was affected.

In addition, it is important to note whether the child's visual impairment exists with another disability. For example, some children with visual impairments also may have developmental or physical impairments. If this is the case, it is necessary to assess each of the child's impairments to assure that all of her needs are receiving the appropriate attention. This chapter focuses specifically on children with only visual impairments.

Although anyone can acquire vision loss after birth, a percentage of children are born blind. *Congenital blindness* can occur from various factors such as fetal exposure to infection or for genetic reasons. Children and adults also can acquire a visual impairment after birth due to a wide spectrum of disorders. For example, an eye injury caused by a sports injury or automobile accident may cause a visual impairment. Other examples of conditions include amblyopia (frequently referred to as lazy eye), cataracts, glaucoma, trachoma, macular degeneration, and retinopathy of prematurity (ROP). In addition, a cortical visual impairment may occur in which the loss of vision results from possible brain damage. For more extensive information about disorders of the eye, consult The National Eye Institute (http://www.nei.nih.gov).

WHAT TEACHERS NEED TO KNOW
ABOUT VISUAL IMPAIRMENTS

Teachers or caregivers often are the first to notice that a child is having difficulty seeing or functioning in her environment due to a possible visual impairment. Some behaviors that children with a visual impairment may demonstrate are:

- rubbing their eyes,
- tilting their head when looking at objects or reading,
- squinting when looking at objects or viewing television,
- holding objects far away from their face, or
- holding objects very close.

If you notice any of these behaviors, it is important to notify the child's family or the school's administrator so the child can get a vision screening. An ophthalmologist or optometrist will make this decision and determine whether additional assessments are necessary.

Once a child receives a comprehensive vision evaluation including a functional assessment of vision "to determine how well a child uses the vision he has in his daily activities in various settings" (Taylor et al., 2008, p. 298), the best educational plan for the child can be determined. Work collaboratively with families, orientation and mobility specialists, healthcare professionals such as ophthalmologists, and visual impairment teachers to design an intervention plan that you can use to help the child to become an active participant in the classroom.

Depending on the severity of the child's visual impairment, the interventions may include the use of assistive technology devices, Braille, books on tape, enlarged print, services with an orientation and mobility specialist, increased activities to improve listening skills, increased use of hands-on materials and manipulatives, preferential seating, and possibly color discrimination activities.

In addition to the modifications to the curriculum and daily activities, assess your physical environment to determine whether alterations are necessary. Depending on the child's visual impairment, and whether or not other disabilities are present, she may be affected by bright colors, specific forms of lighting, glare within the room, the arrangement of furniture (obstacles and barriers that block the child's ability to move freely and safely throughout the room), as well as clutter and visual distractions. Sometimes the weather and the time of day during which the children are participating in activities can have a significant effect on their vision (Gould & Sullivan, 2005).

Again, the decision on how to instruct a child with a visual impairment will depend largely on the type and degree of his impairment and is something to approach collaboratively. The vision teacher and the orientation and mobility specialist are the best sources for obtaining information on modifications and/or accommodations that you can use in the classroom. It especially is important for a child with a visual impairment to be able to move safely throughout his environment.

Keep in mind that many children learn through incidental learning, which means they learn in unplanned situations. For example, social skills training or direct instruction of social skills may be necessary for a child with a visual impairment because he may lack the visual channels necessary to observe interactions. This can lead to deficits in interpersonal communication skills, academic skills, life skills, and self-esteem.

VISUAL IMPAIRMENTS: INCLUSIVE CLASSROOM STRATEGIES

Family Interventions

Professionals can support families who have children with visual impairments by describing strategies for adapting toys, equipment, and furniture in the home. A visit from an orientation and mobility specialist to the child's home may be helpful. In addition, families will appreciate any information you have about assistive technology that they can use in the home.

Classroom Interventions

Some of the recommendations shared below are important for families, but they also are beneficial for use in the classroom.

ADAPTING MATERIALS

For most preschool children with visual impairments, providing opportunities for them to touch, smell, taste (if appropriate), hear, and manipulate materials is sufficient for their knowledge acquisition. As a teacher in the early childhood classroom, you probably already know that both children with special needs and typically developing children learn basic information best through concrete experiences.

You might want to consider making classroom materials that can help children with visual impairments. For example, add textures to the back (or bottom) of attendance tags or use a carpet square with different textures to help children with limited vision. If you use sets of picture cards, outline the shapes using glue so the children can use their sense of touch to identify the shapes, numerals, or alphabet letters. Gather information about commercially prepared materials from the American Printing House for the Blind at http://www.aph.org/catalogs. They design materials specifically for early childhood classrooms. Enlargers or magnifying glasses also can be helpful.

USING BRAILLE

Most preschool classrooms will not have access to Braille materials for children who are legally blind, although some public school classrooms may have such materials. Generally, educators acknowledge that instruction for the blind should be with Braille readers. Braille resources are available through the American Printing House for the Blind mentioned above, as well as the National Library Service for the Blind and Physically Handicapped at http://www.loc.gov/nls. Children with visual impairments typically begin receiving Braille instruction at the kindergarten level in conjunction with beginning reading instruction. There also are picture books with Braille overlays that can be used.

Providing Books on Tape

Children with visual impairments are as capable of enjoying a good story as their sighted peers. A classroom Listening Center stocked with books on CD or tape will be helpful for all children. If you do not have a lot of money in your budget for purchasing books on tape, make your own by recording some of your students' favorite books you already have in the classroom. Additional books are available for purchase at bookstores or through Internet sites.

Working With an Orientation and Mobility Specialist

Orientation and mobility (O&M) skills are part of the curriculum that is included in IEPs for children with visual impairments. The special education and related services team determines the child's specific needs and describes them in the child's IEP or IFSP. An orientation and mobility specialist likely will be involved in providing services to children with visual impairments or blindness. According to Turnbull et al. (2007), the O&M specialist can teach young children how to

- become aware of the spatial layout of their homes and schools,
- listen to the traffic flow in their environment,
- acquire information about environmental sounds, and
- develop spatial and positional concepts.

The O&M specialist works collaboratively with the other service providers and provides support in both the home and school environment. The O&M specialist

provides support to the child as he or she learns to maneuver safely and efficiently in the environment and may also provide support as the child transitions to a new environment, such as a new classroom or even a new home. (Horn, Chambers, & Saito, as cited in Raver, 2009, p. 265)

USING ASSISTIVE TECHNOLOGY

You can find a discussion about assistive technology as an inclusive classroom strategy in Chapter 7 of this book. The use of assistive technology with children who have visual impairments is particularly noteworthy. Among the devices that are available to children with visual impairments are:

- handheld magnifiers (low tech),
- computer screen enlargement systems (high tech),
- computer navigation systems (high tech),
- computer screen readers that use synthesized speech (high tech), and
- Braille embossers (high tech).

Computer navigation systems, computer screen readers, and Braille embossers are essential as children with visual impairments enter the formal educational process. Another high-tech device is an electronic note-taking system. These often have audio output, but they also can generate Braille on an electronic display (Turnbull et al., 2007).

Applying the Strategies

Mrs. Johnson noticed that Emily always moved close to her when she showed materials and objects that the children would use in small groups. She assumed that Emily was probably just a curious child.

Once Emily's teacher, Mrs. Johnson, suspected that Emily had a vision problem, she approached her school administrator about initiating a vision screening for her. Eventually, an early childhood assessment team determined that Emily had "low vision" and developed an IEP for her. Mrs. Johnson was happy to have this plan, because it gave her some direction for working with Emily in her classroom. Some of the accommodations she made for Emily are available below.

WORKING WITH THE WHOLE CLASS

In working with her entire class and classroom, Emily's teacher implemented the following strategies:

- *Rearrange classroom furniture*: Mrs. Johnson scanned the classroom environment and spent some time rearranging the furniture. She moved pieces of furniture or classroom equipment that presented hazards for Emily to locations that would not interfere with Emily when she walked across the room.

- *Talk to the children about how they can help*: As soon as she could, Mrs. Johnson planned a Circle Time to talk about Emily's impairment, and how other children in the group could help Emily move around the classroom. Mrs. Johnson's suggestions included information about how the children should approach Emily and why it was important for the children to identify themselves to Emily. (*Note*: Some controversy exists regarding discussions with peers about specific children's disabilities; however, we feel that if handled with sensitivity, there are many benefits to doing this.)

- *Add tactile materials to classroom items*: Mrs. Johnson evaluated all center materials to determine if she needed to add tactile materials for Emily's use. Mrs. Johnson added a sandpaper strip to the back of Emily's attendance tag so she could identify it by touch. Mrs. Johnson purchased a placemat made of nonskid material to place under puzzle bases, and she located commercial puzzles that play music when the pieces go in the correct places. She also began collecting brightly colored objects, such as beads, pegs, and color tiles, to place in the Manipulatives and Puzzles Center (Gould & Sullivan, 2005).

- *Explain movement activities thoroughly*: When attempting movement activities indoors and outdoors, Mrs. Johnson took the time to carefully explain the movement experience in which the children were to participate. If the children were going to use play equipment, she gave Emily time to explore it with her hands prior to using it. Mrs. Johnson also purchased children's fitness DVDs and CDs to help Emily in developing independence with gross motor activities (Gould & Sullivan, 2005). One CD Mrs. Johnson felt was beneficial was *Aerobic Power for Kids* by Kimbo. Another site that helped her understand children's movement experiences was http://www.kidshealth.org.

♦ *Purchase or make audiobooks:* Mrs. Johnson began ordering books on CD for her classroom from catalogs and Internet Web sites. She recorded herself reading some of the children's favorite books, as well as telling some of their favorite stories to put in the Listening Center.

WORKING WITH THE INDIVIDUAL CHILD

When working one-on-one with Emily, her teacher implemented the following methods:

♦ *Call the child by name:* Mrs. Johnson began calling Emily by name when she wanted her attention. She would identify herself by saying, "Emily, this is Mrs. Johnson speaking." She also remembered to tell Emily when she turned away from her.

♦ *Seat the child close to you:* Emily had already demonstrated her need for preferential seating, so Mrs. Johnson began seating Emily close to her during Circle Time.

♦ *Secure the child's attention:* If Emily's back was toward Mrs. Johnson, Mrs. Johnson would touch Emily on the shoulder to gain her attention. In addition, Ms. Johnson used various tactile and auditory cues to let Emily know what to expect next. For instance, before she would brush Emily's hair, she would gently stroke her hair (tactile) and tell her what was about to occur (auditory).

♦ *Mark center boundaries:* Mrs. Johnson added cookie sheets, trays, and large box lids to the Art Center and to the Manipulatives and Puzzles Center to allow Emily to recognize the center boundaries. This helped her to participate in these two centers (Gould & Sullivan, 2005). By placing the puzzle pieces on the trays or lids, Emily was able to keep the pieces together within the confounds of the trays. The lip of the trays prevented the pieces from falling out of the set area and kept the pieces within her reach.

♦ *Make accommodations for sensory issues:* Mrs. Johnson determined that Emily was squeamish (tactile defensiveness) about playing with playdough in the Art Center, so she placed the playdough inside a resealable plastic bag so Emily could play with it without having to touch it.

♦ *Make use of vision capabilities:* Encourage the child to use the vision that she has. Most children, even if diagnosed as legally blind, have some vision. In order for Ms. Johnson to assist Emily in using her vision, she created larger than normal wall hangings and avoided cluttering areas with a large amount of visual stimuli. This helped Emily to focus on the object of importance.

- *Use hand-over-hand assistance*: Mrs. Johnson recognized Emily's need for hand-over-hand assistance when she had snack or lunch. Initially, Mrs. Johnson asked a parent volunteer to help with this task but eventually, Emily became more independent in her self-help/feeding skills.
- *Use descriptive words*: Mrs. Johnson frequently described the actions of what Emily and her friends were doing. However, Ms. Johnson was careful not to use too many words or sentences. She focused on the key words and actions that impacted Emily.
- *Find helpful resources:* Mrs. Johnson continuously looked for information that would help her learn how to help Emily with her visual impairment. One resource she found that was particularly useful was *The Inclusive Early Childhood Classroom: Easy Ways to Adapt Learning Centers for All Children* by Patti Gould and Joyce Sullivan (2005). This book offered suggestions as to how to adapt the learning center for children with visual impairments as well as for children with other special needs.
- *Consider lighting:* Mrs. Johnson noticed the effects lighting had on Emily's performance. She concluded that Emily struggled when lighting was too intense and changed to softer lighting in the classroom.

Working With Families

When Ms. Johnson talked to Emily's family, the recommendations she made to them included the following:

- *Provide tactile stimulation*: Emily's family provided toys and equipment with more tactilely stimulating surfaces. In addition, many of the toys that Emily's parents provided had auditory output (made noises along with actions).
- *Set defined boundaries*: Emily's family marked the areas that were difficult for Emily to see. For instance, in Emily's home a small table and chairs sits in the corner, which is where Emily keeps her toys. However, the area did not have a clearly defined boundary. Mrs. Johnson suggested to Emily's family that they designate a shelf in her room for her toys. In addition, Emily's table could

have a piece of contrasting tape around it to create a clear border within which Emily could work.

- *Avoid moving objects around*: Mrs. Johnson advised Emily's family to keep things in one place instead of moving objects from one place to another. By keeping objects in clearly defined areas, Emily could easily locate what she needed throughout the day. Emily's family also kept clutter and excess materials out of pathways in which Emily walked.

- *Use hand-over-hand assistance*: Mrs. Johnson suggested that Emily's family use hand-over-hand assistance when Emily requests help. As with all interventions, the assistance should be faded as Emily gains more independence in her skills.

- *Encourage independence*: The teacher encouraged the family to allow Emily to move about and to be as independent as possible, considering her need for safety. The orientation and mobility specialist that serves Emily provided clear guidelines to the family and assisted Emily in moving about her home safely.

SAFETY FIRST

Safety for children with vision impairments, like safety for all children with disabilities, is a high priority. For children who are visually impaired, the following tips are important:

- Use a peer buddy who can guide the child with a visual impairment throughout the normal routine of the day (e.g., during Center Time, when playing outdoors). Because of the responsibility this entails, rotating this classroom task will help children learn about helping others who have special needs. Avoid asking a child who does not want the responsibility of helping the child. Monitor both children during classroom activity to determine that the peer buddy is helping keep the child with visual impairments safe. A peer buddy should never become a substitute for teacher supervision.

- Encourage all children in the classroom to remove clutter from the floor when they see it and store unused toys on shelves, in bins, or in closets. Remind them of this chore on a daily basis. Making sure that chairs are under tables and remain in established spots supports children with visual impairment when they move around the room.

- Instruct children to speak to their peers who have visual impairments and identify themselves prior to touching them to avoid frightening them. Remember to follow this same policy yourself. Children also can learn that they should tell their peer with a visual impairment that they are walking away from him or her.

- If children are riding home with a parent or guardian, supervise them as they get into the car.

- If children are riding on a bus or in a van, supervise them as they get into the vehicle. A parent or guardian should be waiting at the nearest bus stop to help them get off the bus. Walking to the bus is another self-help skill that an orientation and mobility specialist may choose as a goal for a child with a visual impairment. Children with significant impairments to their vision are still able to independently ride a bus with proper instruction and guidance.

- Teach children about safety drills (e.g., fire or tornado). Assign a peer buddy who will always be ready to guide the child with a visual impairment to predetermined areas in case a real emergency occurs (e.g., going outdoors, in case of a fire, or into a protected hallway for tornadoes). Practicing evacuations and drills on a regular basis is important to determine any unforeseen obstacles that may hinder the proper implementation of the drill. Children with visual impairments should be taught to "localize sounds and recognize their source, direction, and distance" (Cook et al., 2008, p. 287).

IF YOU WANT TO KNOW MORE

American Foundation for the Blind
11 Penn Plaza, Ste. 300
New York, NY 10001
800-232-5463
http://www.afb.org

American Printing House for the Blind
1839 Frankfort Avenue
P.O. Box 6085
Louisville, KY 40206-0085
800-223-1839
http://www.aph.org

National Braille Association
95 Allens Creek Road, Bldg. 1, Ste. 202
Rochester, NY 14618
585-427-8260
http://www.nationalbraille.org

National Association for Visually Handicapped
22 West 21st Street, 6th Floor
New York, NY 10010
212-889-3141
http://www.navh.org

National Dissemination Center for Children with Disabilities
1825 Connecticut Ave. NW, Ste. 700
Washington, DC 20009
800-695-0285
http://www.nichcy.org

The National Library Service for the Blind and Physically Handicapped
The Library of Congress
Washington, DC 20542
888-657-7323
http://www.loc.gov/nls

CHAPTER

9

Megan

A CHILD WITH A DEVELOPMENTAL DELAY

"**M**eagan, do you know how to write your name?" asked Mr. Hart, her kindergarten teacher. She held up three fingers and said, "Five year old—I five." Mr. Hart made a second request, "I'm asking you to tell me the letters in your name."

"Five year old—I five," she responded, again holding up three fingers. "One, two, four." Mr. Hart felt sure that Meagan's learning would be difficult during her kindergarten year.

Throughout the school year, Meagan demonstrated a lack of basic skills expected of kindergarten children in her school district. She could not count by rote beyond the numeral three, and counting with meaning was a challenge for her. She could usually count two objects, but beyond that was inaccurate. She also was unable to perform simple addition, even when concrete objects were available for her to use.

Although she tried, she was unable to identify letters of the alphabet except for "M," the first letter of her name. Eventually, she was able to recognize her name on a chart showing her classmates' names, but other words were beyond her ability. By the end of the year, she was able to trace her name, although the size and spacing were not controlled and her letter formation was primitive.

Meagan also attempted to develop positive relationships with others in her class, but she was unskilled with social interactions. Her lack of communication skills prevented her from entering play situations and talking with her classmates, making it difficult for her to achieve more successful social behavior.

When Mr. Hart met with Meagan's mother at the final conference of the year, he told her that Meagan would probably have difficulty the following year in first grade. "She'll need to have a lot of help learning the reading and math skills expected of her in her first year in school."

OVERVIEW OF DEVELOPMENTAL DELAY

When children demonstrate a significant limitation in cognitive functioning, as well as in self-help, communication, and social skills, they will develop more slowly than typically developing peers. When these delays exist, they require further evaluation to determine if the child meets the eligibility criteria for developmental delay. IDEA (1997) provided provisions that permit the use of the category *developmental delay* for children ages birth through 9 for purposes of qualifying for special education services under IDEA. IDEA left the use of developmental delay as an eligibility criteria to the discretion of the state and local agency. Developmental delay under IDEA can include young children with mental retardation, autism, or learning disabilities. However, children over the age of 9 are not eligible by federal law for special education under the eligibility criteria of developmental delay. Older children will be identified through disability categories that often are not appropriate for young children such as mental retardation. The CEC Division for Early Childhood (DEC) stated that "to identify children by traditional disability categories in the early years might result in a premature categorization or miscategorization of children and consequently inappropriate services" (DEC, 2005, p. 1).

In an effort to explain the reasoning behind our decision to include the eligibility criteria of developmental delay in this book, we will examine the traditional eligibility criteria for mental retardation. Although mental retardation is a term that is frequently used, other terms also have been used to describe this condition, including *intellectual disability*, *mental deficiency*, and *intellectually challenged* (Mastropieri & Scruggs, 2010, p. 60). Mental retardation is also referred to as one type of the more general term "developmental disability" (Beirne-Smith, Patton, & Kim, as cited in Mastropieri & Scruggs, 2010, p. 60). There are two primary areas to examine when determining if a child has mental retardation. First, the child must show a limitation in intelligence. Intelligence (IQ) tests measure a person's ability to learn and think. An average score on most IQ tests is a 100. For a person to meet the criteria for mental retardation, he or she must score below the range of 70–75.

In addition, the child must have a limitation in adaptive behavior that comprises three skill types:

- *Conceptual skills*: language and literacy; money, time, and number concepts; and self-direction.
- *Social skills*: interpersonal skills, social responsibility, self-esteem, gullibility, naïveté (i.e., wariness), social problem solving, and the ability to follow rules/obey laws and to avoid being victimized.
- *Practical skills*: activities of daily living (e.g., personal hygiene), occupational skills, healthcare, travel/transportation, schedules/routines, safety, use of money, use of the telephone. (American Association on Intellectual and Developmental Disabilities [AAIDD], 2009)

Deficits in both adaptive behavior and IQ are necessary to meet the criteria for mental retardation. It is important to note that

> in defining and assessing intellectual disability, the American Association on Intellectual and Developmental Disabilities (AAIDD) stresses that professionals must take additional factors into account, such as the community environment typical of the individual's peers and culture. Professionals should also consider linguistic diversity and cultural differences in the way people communicate, move, and behave. (AAIDD, 2009, para. 6)

In very young children, these deficits are difficult to determine because standardized testing, such as IQ testing, is not as strong a predictor of future cognition with young children. Many times, in an attempt to identify a specific diagnostic category for a young child, professionals use standardized and norm-referenced assessments. However, there is question about the psychometric integrity of these instruments. Although a child may exhibit some or all of the characteristics of mental retardation, the validity or reliability of the assessment may be inaccurate due to the young age of the child. Therefore, in this instance, when a child demonstrates the aforementioned characteristics of mental retardation, he or she may not be identified as having mental retardation, but rather identified with a developmental delay. When he or she reaches an age when standardized assessment is more reliable, specialists reevaluate the diagnosis of developmental delay and, in this case, the child may qualify as meeting the eligibility criteria for mental retardation. However, the same child may not meet the criteria for mental retardation and may show only a minor delay and catch up with typically developing peers. This is one of the reasons why federal law (IDEA, 2004) provides states with the option to use the term developmental delay for children between the ages of 3 and 9 years old for special education eligibility purposes. However, the "use of developmental delay should not preclude the use of appropriate disability categories (e.g., visually impaired, deaf-blind)" (DEC, 2005, p. 1).

As previously mentioned, federal law leaves the use of developmental delay for eligibility criteria to the discretion of the state. Despite the recommendation of the DEC (see Appendix A for the DEC position statement, "Developmental Delay as an Eligibility Category"), some states are still inclined to utilize the eligibility criteria of mental retardation (also referred to as intellectual disability) for children exhibiting more severe deficits in development (see above criteria). If teaching a child with special needs in a state that does not utilize this criterion, the child in your classroom, depending on the severity of the delay, may qualify under a different eligibility criteria. For the purposes of providing more inclusive information to the practitioner, the criteria for both mental retardation/intellectual disability and developmental delay will be addressed.

The causes of mental retardation include genetics, prenatal issues, lack of oxygen at birth, and/or other health problems. An example of a genetically based form of mental retardation would be a child who has Down syndrome or Fragile X. A child whose mother drank excessive alcohol during pregnancy may develop fetal alcohol syndrome. Other health problems such as exposure to lead or malnutrition also may cause mental retardation. Research indicates that approximately 2% to 3% of the population has some degree of mental retardation.

The structure of IQ tests classifies individuals with mental retardation as having mild, moderate, severe, and/or profound mental retardation. The severity of the mental retardation will determine the level of help the child needs. For example, a child with mild mental retardation may only experience difficulty learning new information. His ability to learn this new information might be slower than that of his peers. A child with severe mental retardation, on the other hand, may need a significant amount of help learning new things and new skills. This child may grow into adulthood needing long-term support and individualized help. Each person is different and school supports should be determined on the child's strengths and weaknesses rather than his IQ level.

As previously mentioned, some young children may meet some criteria for mental retardation as defined by *DSM-IV-TR*, but not exhibit delays in all areas assessed. This is common in young children who have a difficult time attending to tasks on standardized testing measures. In addition, those children with deficits in cognitive functioning may have a specific learning disability (SLD) as defined by IDEA. However, children typically do not receive a diagnosis of SLD until after the preschool years. Specialists often identify children with cognitive delays that do not meet IDEA's definition for mental retardation or learning disabilities as having a developmental delay. These children receive a reevaluation at a future date when there is a better opportunity to assess their cognitive abilities. This identification label is given to children between the ages of 3 and 9 and at the discretion of the state in which the child is assessed.

A more specific definition for developmental delay is defined by DEC (2005) as:

> a condition which represents a significant delay in the process of development. It does not refer to a condition in which a child is slightly or momentarily lagging in development. The presence of developmental delay is an indication that the process of development is significantly affected and that without special intervention; it is likely that educational performance at school age will be affected. (p. 1)

Controversy exists over the appropriate terminology to use with children who exhibit intellectual/cognitive/developmental impairments. For example, many times a family member may be told that her child has a developmental delay, then a year later the same child meets eligibility criteria for mental retardation. Regardless of whether or not the term *mental retardation* is deemed appropriate to use, this specific terminology has and continues to be used in federal legislation. Many experts in the field of special education prefer to utilize the term *developmental disability* to either mental retardation or intellectual disabilities. The reasoning behind this is that developmental disability reflects a wide variety of conditions that are a direct result from a myriad of causes that emerge between birth and 18 years of age, the developmental period (Taylor et al., 2008). It is not our intent to determine which term to use, but rather to share strategies and information that will be helpful in including a child who exhibits any form of cognitive impairment (either mental retardation or developmental delay). The remainder of this chapter will use the term developmental delay, as this term is the one most recently adopted by professionals in the field of early childhood special education. In the public school system, developmental delay as an eligibility criteria often is preferred to mental retardation prior to age 6.

WHAT TEACHERS NEED TO KNOW ABOUT CHILDREN WITH A DEVELOPMENTAL DELAY

Often young children go undiagnosed with mild forms of developmental delays. Detecting a specific form of a developmental delay can be difficult if a child does not demonstrate the distinctive physical characteristics associated with mental retardation (e.g., chromosomal characteristics, such as Down syndrome). Many teachers find that the initial diagnoses in young children occur when they are enrolled in a program for 3- to 4-year-olds. Signs that a child may have a developmental delay that you might observe include difficulty with:

- learning to communicate or talk,
- following directions,
- social interactions and social cues,
- taking care of hygiene needs (bathroom and dressing),
- feeding himself and drinking independently, and
- short- and long-term memory and performing actions without regard to consequences.

In addition, toddlers with developmental delays tend to show a delay in the acquisition of language and very young children may lag behind typically developing peers in sitting, crawling, walking, or running (gross motor skills).

It is important to note that young children develop very rapidly during infancy and the toddler years. Many delays are merely a child progressing through developmental stages at a slower pace than his peers, but not necessarily with a significant delay. Only a professional can make the determination of specific developmental delays. However, information obtained from family members, caregivers, and teachers is a critical component in the assessment process.

Children diagnosed with specific intellectual disabilities, such as developmental delay or mental retardation, prior to the age of 3 are provided with support services through Early Childhood Intervention (ECI) programs. The ECI service supports families' as well as children's specific needs. It is possible to implement many of the services ECI provides at the childcare facility. As when working with all children with special needs, it is necessary to collaborate with professionals. Teachers also should be aware of the individual needs of the child when making the appropriate adaptations to the curriculum. For example, a child with a delay in self-help skills may need more support and encouragement when engaged in social interactions or when "playing dress up" in the home setting. He or she may need specific modeling of how to dress up or need to have a teacher provide prompting to elicit language during the role-playing processes (further explanations of specific strategies are provided below).

DEVELOPMENTAL DELAY: INCLUSIVE CLASSROOM STRATEGIES

Family Interventions

Although most of the interventions described in this chapter are more appropriate for classroom practice, families need information about helping their children develop social skills, encouraging their independence, and providing concrete demonstrations of new learning. You can disseminate information in these areas by sharing with families the classroom strategies that you use on a daily basis. In addition, it is of critical importance that families are provided with the recommended practices for improving practices for young children with special needs and their families found on the Council for Exceptional Children's Division for Early Childhood Web site (http://www.dec-sped.org).

Critics of the term developmental delay argue that this term sends a false message to parents that their child is only delayed in acquiring a specific skill and that she will catch up with her peers soon. Special attention to parents' perceptions of their child's disability should be given. If a teacher sees this as an obstacle in providing an effective intervention plan, a school psychologist may be of assistance. The school psychologist can review assessment findings and share with the parents both the child's strengths and weaknesses as well as the need to look at intervention planning based on the child's individual needs.

Classroom Interventions

Mr. Hart's approach to working with Meagan included many of the following strategies to enhance her abilities to develop cognitively.

PROVIDING INDIVIDUALIZED INSTRUCTION

When children learn at a slower pace than their classmates, you must provide them with additional instruction and opportunities to practice skills they acquire. Individual attention from you, parent volunteers, or high school student organization members who help in the classroom benefits children with developmental delays. Volunteers can help with tasks such as helping children learn to count, remember their alphabet letters, recognize shapes, retell stories, how to tie their shoes, put puzzles together, and play classroom games (e.g., Concentration or Go Fish). Teachers can determine the best way to utilize classroom helpers by learning about the specific developmental delay the child has and understanding the deficits that need to be addressed. You can observe children to determine the types of activities they need in one-on-one settings and plan for the volunteers to give them assistance.

INSTRUCTING CHILDREN ON SOCIAL SKILLS

Social skills instruction is the same as social skills training, which is described in Chapter 4 (please refer to Chapter 4 for a detailed discussion). With children who have developmental delays, social skills instruction improves with concrete demonstrations of social learning and asking children to role-play social situations to help them learn to understand others' perspectives, negotiate, take turns, share with others, and understand democratic practices (Warner & Lynch, 2004). Using social stories and social scripts provides another avenue to teach social skills to children with developmental delays (see pp. 47–49 for additional information on social stories).

OFFERING CONCRETE DEMONSTRATIONS OF NEW LEARNING

Children with developmental delays benefit by seeing concrete demonstrations of the skills they should acquire. For example, if you want children to place a series of attribute blocks (blocks designed with various shapes, colors, and thicknesses) in a specific pattern (e.g., red, yellow, blue, red, yellow, blue), sit with those children and show them how to make the pattern by forming the pattern first. Showing the children how to do the activity several times and then providing other patterns of blocks for them to match will help them gradually gain independence in performing this task. Monitor children as they move toward independence, and be prepared to step in if they appear frustrated. Starting again may be necessary if children fail to understand what they should be doing.

USING SIGNALS TO PROMPT TASKS

Many skills that children acquire through social interactions may not be as easily acquired by children with developmental delays. Using a simple cueing system, such as a hand signal, will help the child recognize it is time to engage in a social response. For example, when teaching a child to take turns, he or she must be aware of the social cue indicating it is time to talk or have a turn. If this is not naturally occurring, a teacher or caregiver can provide a hand signal that indicates it is time to take a turn.

ENCOURAGING INDEPENDENCE

All children need to participate independently in activities. Children with developmental delays may require help with a wide range of experiences, from dressing themselves and setting a table for snack to acquiring social and academic skills. Using a step-by-step instructional strategy and breaking down the task (task analysis) helps children to accomplish skills. Show children how to do activities or use pictures of children doing the same activity. This will help them remember how to complete the tasks. For example, if you want children to cut out a heart shape from folded construction paper, show them how to do it (model the task) and then monitor them as they do it, giving them positive feedback about their achievement.

Using Task Analysis

Children with developmental delays will benefit from instructional practices that include task analysis. Specific skills can be complex. Task analysis is when you break a skill into smaller steps. After determining the specific steps that are required to perform the task, each individual step is demonstrated to the child. The child then completes the specific step with your assistance. When one step is completed the next step in the task is introduced. The sequencing of the individual steps will lead to the competition of the task. The smaller steps should be taught sequentially. The attention span of the child and his cognitive abilities should be considered when determining the level of support to provide during the process and the number of steps that will be necessary for teaching the desired skill.

Making Anecdotal Records

Anecdotal records are observational records that teachers use to indicate a pattern in children's behavior or knowledge acquisition. If you suspect any form of developmental delay, keep a daily record (similar to a journal or diary) describing the child's behavior in social and cognitive areas. This will help when you when recommending screenings or assessments. For example, if an entry on Friday indicates that a child does not remember an event that happened on Monday, this would provide the necessary information needed to make an adequate judgment about the child's ability to learn. Here are sample anecdotal records for a child named Zoey:

> 2/17—Zoey appeared to be confused today when I asked her to count to five. I provided buttons for her to count, but she did not seem to know how to begin. She could only count to three with prompting.
> 2/21—Zoey counted to five easily this morning as I prompted her, but she was unable to begin when I asked her again to perform the same task.

2/22—I suggested to Zoey's family that they help her at home with her counting skills. I asked them to concentrate only on counting to five.

2/27—Still no success with Zoey's ability to count to five independently.

2/28—Zoey came to school today with a grin on her face. She told me that she could count and then demonstrated her ability to count to three all by herself. Her family has been working with her! I'll check again next week to see if she remembers this skill.

REPEATING INSTRUCTION

Repetition is an excellent instructional strategy that can benefit many children. Some children with developmental delays will need to have specific directions or information repeated often. In addition, after repeating instructions, you should check that the child understands them. This also holds true with providing multiple opportunities for a child to practice skills.

STRUCTURING INSTRUCTION

In an inclusive classroom, typically developing children often serve as models for children with specific disabilities. Teachers can structure learning activities to incorporate the use of peers as models. Allowing children to work in small groups often facilitates this type of structured activity. For example, if the children are working on puzzles in the classroom, a small group can be assigned to work at a table. The level of the puzzles may be different (more or fewer pieces per child), but the action necessary to complete the task (i.e., putting the puzzle together) is the same. The child with a developmental delay will be working side-by-side with his typically developing peers and will see how the task is performed by his peer. In addition, children in small groups often will help each other in the learning process (this is called peer instruction).

Applying the Strategies

When Mr. Hart met with Meagan's mother at the final conference of the year, he told her that Meagan would probably have difficulty the following year in first grade. "She will need to have a lot of help learning the reading and math skills expected of her in her first year in school."

Mr. Hart recognized rather quickly in the school year that Meagan was learning at a slower pace than the rest of her classmates. Although he was not sure that she had an intellectual disability, he decided to follow a course of action that would allow him to learn as much as he possibly could about her abilities. The outlines of some of the procedures he followed are available below.

WORKING WITH THE WHOLE CLASS

When considering his entire class and classroom, Mr. Hart utilized the following strategies:

- *Model center activities*: Mr. Hart recognized that he would need to model many of the center activities for Meagan. Before she played in the Block Center, he demonstrated how to enter the play area and how to build simple structures. As Meagan first began to play, Mr. Hart provided her with only a small number of blocks (five or six) so that she would not become overwhelmed.
- *Engage in explicit teaching strategies*: Children with developmental delays often need opportunities for learning specific tasks through deliberate or planned strategies. Many specific strategies that are discussed throughout this book fall into the explicit teaching category. For example, prompts (e.g., physical, verbal, visual, gestural, modeling) and cues (e.g., specific command or direction indicating a response is needed) are two types of strategies. "Prompts and cues are among the actions teachers can take to help children learn behaviors or responses needed to participate in early learning contexts with their peers" (Winter, 2007, p. 291). Winter (2007) defined specific prompts and cues as follows:
  - *Cue*: a command or direction that helps a child know a response is necessary
  - *Physical or manual prompts*: the providing of physical assistance to cue a child to respond accordingly. This type of prompt is also called hand-over-hand prompting
  - *Verbal prompts*: the use of words or voice inflictions to help a child gain information
  - *Visual prompts*: the use of pictures, words, or graphics to convey information or help a child learn concepts

- *Gestural prompts*: the use of nonverbal signs or gestures to convey information and invite responses
- *Modeling*: the demonstrating of desired performance or set of behaviors (p. 291)

Working With Individual Children

In working one-on-one with Meagan, Mr. Hart implemented the following techniques:

- *Keep anecdotal records and have frequent informal assessments*: Mr. Hart began writing anecdotal records (see the section in this chapter titled "Classroom Interventions" for more information about anecdotal records) at the end of each day as a reminder to himself about how Meagan was responding to classroom learning experiences. Mr. Hart also began keeping a record of Meagan's ability to remember information that he had introduced during class in previous days and weeks. He met with her two or three times a week for an informal assessment of what she remembered from earlier lessons (such as naming shapes or colors or recalling basic facts about a unit they had studied).

- *Work with child individually to manage behavior*: As Mr. Hart began to acquire more information about the various forms of intellectual disabilities, he learned that children with deficits in cognitive abilities often demonstrate behavioral difficulties. Although Meagan was amiable most of the time, Mr. Hart noticed that Meagan grew frustrated when she felt challenged with activities that were difficult for her. Meagan was unable to put most of the classroom puzzles together, and she often forgot how to tie her shoes. Mr. Hart felt his intervention would become important in preventing serious social problems, so he continued to work with her on an individual basis at every chance he could manage. He also encouraged her family to work on the same skills he was trying to enforce.

- *Provide detailed step-by-step procedures*: Meagan performed much more efficiently when Mr. Hart organized instruction in step-by-step procedures. For example, if Meagan said that she wanted to paint a picture at the easel in the Art Center, Mr. Hart accompanied her so he could provide instructions. Mr. Hart also selected a large easel for the classroom, which helped Meagan use large arm movements while painting. Below is an example of his step-by-step instructions:

1. "Meagan, put on a paint apron to help you stay clean."
2. "Now, put art paper on the easel." This encouraged Meagan's independence. Be prepared to provide assistance (e.g., with masking tape to hold the paper in place), but let the child try to complete the task on her own.
3. Pointing to the paintbrushes in the paint jars on the easel tray, Mr. Hart reminded Meagan to change brushes when she changed paint colors.
4. While circulating around the room, Mr. Hart monitored Meagan as she painted. Periodically, he made comments about the colors she used and told her how much he enjoyed her attempt at easel painting.
5. When Meagan was finished with her work, Mr. Hart showed her the clothesline and clothespins she could use to let her painting dry. "Meagan, please hang your work here and then put your apron in the box." This resulted in Meagan feeling a sense of accomplishment and independence.

- *Modify fine motor activities for the child*: When Meagan chose fine motor activities, Mr. Hart provided cardboard box lids to help her confine her materials in one space. He substituted glue sticks for glue bottles because it was difficult for Meagan to judge how much glue to use (Gould & Sullivan, 2005). He also placed his hand on hers when she was working on a difficult task such as stringing beads. Consequently, she felt more comfortable with her attempts to put beads on the string.
- *Prepare the child for transitions*: Meagan needed help understanding transitions to other activities so Mr. Hart always told her a few minutes ahead of time what would happen next. "Meagan," he would say, "In 5 minutes, it will be snack time. We clean up before snack. I'll ring a bell when it's time to clean up." Mr. Hart learned that Meagan needed additional time for transitioning than her peers, so he approached her each time to provide individual instruction.
- *Plan for restlessness and inattentiveness during Circle Time*: Meagan often fidgeted during Circle Time. Mr. Hart provided her with a

toy to engage her when the group had daily Circle Time. When it appeared that Meagan could not pay attention for more than a few minutes, a classroom volunteer would take her to another part of the room to read her a book or to do an art activity. Mr. Hart often planned movement activities during Circle Time because Meagan responded well to them. Sometimes he noticed that Meagan would refocus when he asked all of the children to stand, turn around, and sit back down.

- *Develop the child's ability to focus*: Throughout the year, Mr. Hart encouraged Meagan to participate in activities for increasingly longer periods. He would often say, "Just do one more, and then you can stop." Eventually, Meagan's ability to focus on a task increased to the typical range of expectations for kindergarteners.

- *Monitor pacing*: Mr. Hart was aware that Meagan needed additional time to process newly acquired information. He would allow for extended times in activities and presented new information in smaller increments and over a longer period of time.

WORKING WITH FAMILIES

Mr. Hart utilized the following methods when working with Meagan's family to ensure a school-to-home connection:

- *Recommend early childhood intervention resources to child's family*: Mr. Hart recommended that Meagan's family contact the early childhood intervention team in their community for assessment. This team might help the family in getting a hearing and vision screening for her. Children should receive a hearing and vision screening prior to determining if a developmental delay exists. Children often receive referrals for evaluations to determine if cognitive deficits are present. During the evaluation process, they find that the child has a vision problem and needs glasses. The vision problem may be the reason why the child is not performing at the same level as her peers. It is important to rule out vision and hearing impairments first.

- *Suggest that the child be evaluated for developmental delay*: Because Meagan is in kindergarten and 5 years old, she is entitled to receive special education services through the public school system, including a full evaluation if she has a developmental delay. The assessment would determine what additional services

Meagan would need to help her be more successful in school. If Meagan had been younger (birth to 2 years), federal law would also provide opportunities to receive services, as necessary, by early childhood intervention programs.

- *Communicate with families about concepts learned at school*: Mr. Hart made sure to communicate with Meagan's family about important concepts that the children were learning each week so that they could reinforce his instruction at home. If he had been teaching about counting to 10 by twos, for example, her family worked with her at home to make sure she was acquiring the necessary content.

- *Maintain regular contact with all families*: As a matter of course, Mr. Hart sent out regular newsletters to the families of the children in his classroom. One section of the newsletter emphasized concepts that the children were learning while they were at school.

- *Have regular conferences with the child's family*: Mr. Hart's conferences with Meagan's family included information about preparing her for transitional activities, providing step-by-step procedures, helping her with managing her own behavior (he shared several fact sheets with the family), and modifying fine motor activities for her use. The American Academy of Child and Adolescent Psychiatry has several family resources including Facts for Families, a one-page fact sheet on specific topics that teachers can provide to families to help communicate the school-to-home learning of skills (available at http://www.aacap.org/cs/root/facts_for_families/facts_for_families). Fact sheets are packets professional organizations generate to provide families, professionals, and other interested persons with summarized information about various disabilities.

SAFETY FIRST

As mentioned in previous chapters, safety for all children is a high priority in any classroom. For Meagan and other children with developmental delays, the following tips are important:

- Remind children about appropriate behaviors in the classroom to avoid excessive running or other movements that might cause accidents.

- Remember to repeat instructions for children with intellectual disabilities when everyone is leaving the classroom to go to another spot in the building or when going outdoors, even if you have told them these same instructions many times before. Remind them about safety on playground equipment and how to play appropriately on various pieces of equipment.
- If children are riding home with a family member, supervise them as they get into the car.
- If they are riding on a bus (or in a van), supervise them as they get into the vehicle. A family member should be waiting at the nearest bus stop to help them get off the bus.
- Teach children about safety drills (e.g., fire and tornado). As opportunities arise, take time to practice these drills so children will be well prepared in case of a real emergency.

IF YOU WANT TO KNOW MORE

American Association on Intellectual and Developmental Disabilities
501 3rd St., NW, Ste. 200
Washington, DC 20001
800-424-3688
http://www.aaidd.org

The Arc of the United States
1010 Wayne Avenue, Ste. 650
Silver Spring, MD 20910
800-433-5255
http://www.thearc.org

Council for Exceptional Children (CEC) Division for Early Childhood (DEC)
27 Fort Missoula Road, Ste. 2
Missoula, MT 59804
406-543-0872
http://www.dec-sped.org

CHAPTER 10

Mollie

A CHILD WITH TRAUMATIC BRAIN INJURY

"**M**s. Cooke, my head hurts," Mollie said as she held her hand over her left ear. Melody Cooke recognized Mollie's statement as one more in a series of symptoms that described Mollie's traumatic brain injury (TBI), the result of an accident in her home. Because Mollie held her hand over her ear when she complained about pain, Ms. Cooke made a note to herself to talk to Mollie's family about whether Mollie had received a hearing screening since her accident or whether she had an ear infection recently.

Several months had elapsed since Mollie's mother had told Ms. Cooke about the accident and the family's subsequent trip to the emergency room. Mollie had hit her head on the pavement in front of her home when she fell out of a wagon her older sister was pushing. Although initially her injury did not appear to be severe (not an open head injury), Mollie's classroom functioning had changed as a result of the fall. Knowing that Mollie had been diagnosed with TBI made Ms. Cooke more conscious and alert to symptoms that may occur later due to the accident.

Ms. Cooke noticed that Mollie's inability to remember some of the information she had previously learned was creating frustration for her. She also seemed less attentive and occasionally demonstrated behavioral problems when asked to sit still during Circle Time. When Ms. Cooke asked Mollie questions, she often appeared not to hear and did not respond well throughout the normal routine activities of the school day.

Ms. Cooke also observed that Mollie, who had been friendly and cheerful prior to her accident, did not seem to interact with her peers as easily as she once did. Mollie seemed unable to talk to them coherently, so she resorted to hitting and pushing other children to get what she wanted. Mollie's communication skills had deteriorated, and she often had a hard time remembering what she wanted to say and saying it quickly enough for others to understand. Ms. Cooke kept careful records of what was occurring in the classroom and shared them with Mollie's family. This information was essential in helping Mollie's physician determine what types of long- and short-term effects the accident would have on her.

OVERVIEW OF TRAUMATIC BRAIN INJURY

Unlike many of the special needs discussed in this book, traumatic brain injury (TBI) often can occur overnight with little or no warning to the family or person involved. TBI also differs from many other special needs as prevention strategies are available that can greatly reduce the risk of obtaining a TBI (e.g., wearing a helmet when riding a bicycle, wearing a seatbelt while riding in an automobile). Taking safety precautions might reduce the possibility of suffering from a TBI if an accident were to occur.

Traumatic brain injury is a complex injury. IDEA (2004) defined it as

an acquired injury to the brain caused by an external physical force, resulting in total or partial functional disability or psychological impairment, or both, that adversely affects a child's educational performance. The term applies to open or closed head injuries resulting in impairments in one or more areas, such as cognition; language; memory; attention; reasoning; abstract thinking; judgment; problem solving; sensory, perceptual and motor abilities; psycho-social behavior; physical functions; information processing; and speech. The term does not apply to brain injuries that are congenital or degenerative, or to brain injuries induced by birth trauma. (IDEA, 2004, 34 Code of Federal Regulations 300.7(c)(12))

Specialists classify traumatic brain injuries as either open or closed head injuries. Closed head injuries occur more frequently than open head injuries. When specifically discussing TBI, a closed head injury occurs when an impact or strike to the head injures the brain but leaves the skull intact. The skull itself withstands the impact or collusion, but the brain becomes damaged. In this case; there is no fracturing of the bones of the skull. The degree of damage will depend on the strength and force of the impact. An example of a cause for this type of TBI is a car accident where the head forcefully hits the dashboard.

Open head injuries are less common injuries to the brain. They occur when a part of the skull or a foreign object (such as a bullet) penetrates the brain. When the skull penetrates the brain, bacteria can enter and possibly cause impairments within the affected part of the brain.

Car accidents cause approximately half of all reported cases of TBI. Other causes involve gunshot wounds, motorcycle accidents, sports injuries, falls, and child abuse. Young children and infants can incur TBI when they are vigorously shaken, commonly referred to as shaken baby syndrome. Many complications can occur with TBI including coma, seizures, infections, nerve damage, cognitive disabilities, sensory problems, difficulty swallowing, language difficulties, personality changes, and, possibly, Alzheimer's or Parkinson's disease (MayoClinic.com, 2006).

The extent to which an individual will display complications will range from mild to severe depending on the degree and severity of the TBI. When a child suffers from a head injury, that child requires a full comprehensive exam by a team of specialists to assess not just physical injuries, but cognitive, behavioral, and developmental domains as well. The assessment will most likely consist of a computerized tomography (CT) or computerized axial tomography (CAT) san. Some physicians also will do a positron emission tomography (PET) scan. Often, physicians provide neurological testing as well to determine deficits in various processing skills.

The age of onset, area of the brain affected, and the severity of the TBI will determine changes in cognitive functioning and the individual's long-term prognosis. Taylor et al. (2008) grouped the characteristics of TBI into four main areas:

1. *Cognitive*: Including, but not limited to, language comprehension, concentration, attention, judgment, and possible decrease in intelligence.
2. *Physical*: Including, but not limited to, problems with walking, speaking, coordination, hearing, onset of seizures, and paralysis.

3. *Behavioral, social, and emotional*: Including, but not limited to, attention deficits, mood changes, impulsivity, loss of emotional control, outbursts, and difficulty maintaining conversations.
4. *Academic functioning*: Including, but not limited to, reading comprehension and decoding skills.

Often with TBI, concerns in these areas do not appear immediately after the accident. Signs of problems may begin to surface several months or years after an accident occurs. Due to a possible delay in the characteristics, careful tracking of a child's behaviors once TBI has been determined is necessary.

Unfortunately, many of the symptoms of TBI mirror those symptoms of attention deficit disorder, behavior disorders, mild mental retardation, and learning disabilities. This often leads to a misdiagnosis, possibly resulting in interventions that prove unsuccessful. Although families and even teachers can observe many symptoms of TBI, children receive the actual diagnosis of TBI only after a complete medical examination.

WHAT TEACHERS NEED TO KNOW ABOUT TRAUMATIC BRAIN INJURY

You should be aware that TBI often occurs suddenly, impacting children and families at a rapid, unexpected rate. Family members often will seek the support of the school or childcare facility when determining the best learning environment for their child. Often caregivers find themselves offering emotional support to parents as they struggle to deal with this unexpected event. Collaborating with the family of a child with TBI is essential.

In addition to offering emotional support, keep in mind that most frequently, symptoms of severe TBI will occur immediately or shortly after the injury has occurred. However, in some cases (such as in a mild injury), less obvious symptoms may occur at a later date. If a family member indicates that a child has had a blow to the head or has fallen, several symptoms may occur that you should report to the family, including:

◆ headaches,
◆ dizziness,

- confusion,
- mood changes,
- excessive tiredness,
- muscle tightness,
- trouble holding a conversation,
- memory problems,
- uncontrolled emotions,
- concentration problems,
- slurred speech,
- seizures,
- change in coordination, and
- lack of motivation.

Many of the characteristics above may occur in typically developing children and not warrant concern; however, if the symptoms are not typical of the child's normal behavior and the family has notified you of a recent fall or injury, medical help may be necessary. In addition, if loss of consciousness, confusion, and/or seizures occur, the facility's emergency plan should be implemented. This is especially important to recognize if these symptoms come on suddenly after a fall or injury.

As a result of TBI, many of the child's skills can diminish. The child may even need to relearn functional living skills. Remembering information and learning new tasks can be difficult for a child or adult suffering from TBI. She may experience problems with coordination, speaking, hearing, and energy levels. Her behavior may change from how it was before the accident.

Types of behavioral changes reported in children with TBI include temper outbursts, irritability, hyperactivity, lack of self-control, and increased aggressiveness. Mood swings and lack of emotional control also may be present. Academically, a child who previously did not have problems with learning may experience problems with word retrieval, written language, comprehension, and decoding (Taylor et al., 2008).

This sudden change in a child's daily functions poses its own set of challenges in the classroom. You might find it difficult to change the expectations you have for the child. This holds especially true when physical limitations are not present.

Because children with TBI have varying needs based on the severity as well as the location of their injuries, it is difficult to determine the degree of support a child will need and the long- and short-term implications. Children with TBI may exhibit all or none of the symptoms examined above. However, the following section will address some common interventions and ideas that you can implement in the classroom setting. Keep in mind that the classification of TBI can be challenging for early interventionists,

> particularly in regard to understanding the nature of recovering from a traumatic brain injury as well as specialized rehabilitation and intervention techniques. It is especially important to coordinate services with medical personnel who can provide guidance relative to safety issues and supportive therapies. (Hooper & Umansky, 2009, p. 33)

TRAUMATIC BRAIN INJURY: INCLUSIVE CLASSROOM STRATEGIES

Family Interventions

Collaborating with the special education and related services team is as important when working with children who have traumatic brain injury as with other children who have special needs. Most children with a severe traumatic brain injury are hospitalized for a period of time and work with a rehabilitation team, along with their families. This team may include a physiatrist (a medical doctor who specializes in physical medicine and rehabilitation), rehabilitation nurse, neuropsychologist (someone who studies children's abilities to remember and use language), physical therapist, and/or occupational therapist.

Classroom Interventions

Some of the inclusive classroom strategies for TBI are similar to those discussed previously in the chapters on ADHD (see Chapter 4) and developmental delay (see Chapter 9). Common among these strategies are: behavior modification (discussed in Chapter 4), and anecdotal records, concrete demonstrations of new learning, task analysis, and individualized instruction (described in Chapter 9). Other strategies are presented in the following sections.

Working With the Home-School Liaison

Ms. Cooke became aware of all of the services the home-school liaison was able to offer her. She received information about:

- daily living, mobility, and orientation skills that Mollie might need;
- how to assess her language level and accommodations to her language needs;
- helping improve Mollie's listening skills; and
- how to increase her ability to remember and learn.

The school reentry specialist enhanced Ms. Cooke's expertise with individualized instruction. Mollie soon was the recipient of Ms. Cooke's new knowledge.

Working With the Child's Related Services Team

Teachers should be prepared to work with many related services providers. A few of these are particularly important when working with children with TBI. They include:

- *Hospital-school liaison*: The hospital-school liaison, often referred to as a school reentry specialist, is a great resource to help you understand the child's needs. The main responsibility of the hospital-school liaison is to keep school personnel informed of the child's progress in rehabilitation and make provisions for homebound instruction, if necessary (Turnbull et al., 2007).
- *Speech-language pathologists*: Speech-language pathologists provide speech therapy for children with traumatic brain injuries who need help relearning language or improving language skills that the injury affected. Occasionally, children attend therapy sessions while in school, but they also may occur at other sites away from the school or center.
- *Physical therapists*: Physical therapists assess children's balance, strength, movement, and need for equipment (e.g., a wheelchair or brace). They provide training to individuals who need to regain their abilities to walk and move more normally. Sometimes, they need to assist with pain management techniques. Usually the assistance they provide will be in settings other than the classroom or school, but you can learn techniques from them that will be beneficial in the classroom.

- *Occupational therapists*: Occupational therapists assess functions and complications related to the child's daily living skills, cognition, and vision and perception, all of which a traumatic brain injury may affect. They help the child determine the best ways to perform daily living skills and personal hygiene needs. If required, occupational therapists will identify any equipment the child may need at school (e.g., for eating) or at home (e.g., for dressing and bathing). Consult with the child's occupational therapists to help you develop plans to help implement daily skills for children with traumatic brain injury.

Depending on the specific type of TBI the child in your classroom has, additional related service personnel may be involved in his or her IEP or IFSP.

Applying the Strategies

Ms. Cooke noticed almost immediately after her injury that Mollie's inability to remember some of the information she had previously learned was creating frustration for her. She also seemed less attentive and occasionally demonstrated behavioral problems when asked to sit still during Circle Time. When Ms. Cooke asked Mollie questions, she often appeared not to hear and did not respond well throughout the normal routine activities of the school day.

Ms. Cooke was able to observe Mollie's daily behaviors and actions at school in light of her knowledge of Mollie's accident, providing valuable information to Mollie's families and doctors. She also implemented several changes in her classroom to accommodate for the changes in Mollie's learning and abilities. These are described below.

WORKING WITH THE WHOLE CLASS

Ms. Cooke implemented the following strategies when considering her entire class and classroom:
- *Maintain consistent routines*: Ms. Cooke recognized that consistent routines were necessary with all children and specifically with Mollie to prevent her from becoming frustrated or anxious when change occurred in the classroom schedule. Ms. Cooke made sure to warn Mollie of upcoming transitions throughout the day. All preschoolers need daily activities that are predictable and

consistent, but children with traumatic brain injuries are more likely to react negatively to disruptions in the schedule. (You can find more information about consistent routines in Chapter 3.)

- *Encourage children to practice new skills*: Ms. Cooke gave the children numerous opportunities to practice new skills. She often encouraged Mollie to practice skills that she had acquired. For example, Ms. Cooke would sit with Mollie and ask her to retell stories or demonstrate how to put objects into groups of two. Then Ms. Cooke would give Mollie feedback about her achievements: "You really knew that story well!" or "Let's count how many groups you've made."

- *Plan daily movement experiences*: Ms. Cooke planned for daily movement experiences for the entire class in order to help the students with balance, posture, and mobility. Her classroom did not have a balance beam, so she placed a 6' long, 2" x 4" plank on the floor for all children to balance on as they walked on it. Children with TBI benefit from movement activities, not only physically, but mentally as well.

WORKING WITH INDIVIDUAL CHILDREN

Ms. Cooke's concern for Mollie led her to make the following accommodations in her classroom to ensure Mollie was in the least restrictive environment:

- *Keep anecdotal records*: Ms. Cooke began keeping anecdotal records of Mollie's behavior in her classroom as soon as she learned of Mollie's accident. Ms. Cooke knew that her observations were necessary to keep Mollie's family and her rehabilitation team informed about Mollie's progress. Noting relapses in her behavior or other symptoms as they appeared was important to helping Mollie deal with her disability. (Please see Chapter 9 for information about keeping anecdotal records.)

- *Give the child individual instruction*: Ms. Cooke began a systematic approach to help Mollie understand new information presented to the group. Ms. Cooke planned time for individual instruction, giving step-by-step directions about accomplishing tasks (e.g., putting puzzles together, forming patterns, completing art projects) and demonstrating how to do new classroom activities.

- *Assess the child's acquisition of skills often*: Ms. Cooke also began a systematic approach in assessing Mollie's acquisition of skills. Most of the time, Ms. Cooke would observe Mollie as she completed tasks to determine her skill, but sometimes Ms. Cooke would make a special request: "Mollie, come talk to me about how you put these Legos® together," or "I would like to see you separate these dollhouse furniture pieces into categories."
- *Eliminate unnecessary distractions (if possible)*: As Ms. Cooke became aware of Mollie's reactions to distractions in the classroom (e.g., loud noises, groups of children outside the classroom), she attempted to eliminate as many of the distractions as she could. She talked to her entire class about "indoor voices" and "outdoor voices," encouraging them to use quieter voices when they talked in the classroom. She modeled this behavior herself. Ms. Cooke also talked to other teachers in her school about moving away from the building when their children were outdoors to cut down on the noise factor that distracted several of her children.
- *Provide opportunities for the child to rest*: Mollie seemed to tire more easily than she had prior to her accident. Particularly during the months following her accident, Ms. Cooke made sure to provide opportunities for Mollie to rest. Ms. Cooke placed a small tent in a quiet corner in her classroom with a blanket and pillow to encourage Mollie to nap if she wanted. Ms. Cooke told all of the children in the classroom that anyone could use this new Rest Center if they needed to rest.
- *Remain patient*: The concern for Mollie that Ms. Cooke felt often tugged at her heartstrings because she recognized that Mollie was not performing as well as she had prior to her accident. Nevertheless, Ms. Cooke reminded herself to be patient and allow as much latitude as possible in her expectations about what Mollie could and could not do while she was at school.
- *New learning*: Although Molly still had the knowledge and skills that she had developed prior to the accident, Ms. Cooke tried to keep in mind that new learning of skills would likely be slow for Mollie.

After Mollie's injury occurred, her teacher worked to ensure communication with the family, using the following strategies:

- *Research TBI*: Utmost in Ms. Cooke's mind was her own need to find out as much as she could about TBI and how she could help Mollie while Mollie was in her classroom. Ms. Cooke began searching the Internet (some of the resources appear at the end of this chapter) and reading as much as she could about traumatic brain injury. She made sure to pass the information along to Mollie's family.

- *Communicate with the family*: When Ms. Cooke became aware of skills that Mollie was having difficulty acquiring, Ms. Cooke notified Mollie's family quickly. During conferences with Mollie's mother, Ms. Cooke gave her as many tips as possible for improving Mollie's skills acquisition.

SAFETY FIRST

When you have a child in your classroom with a traumatic brain injury, the following tips are critical to ensuring his or her safety:

- Be prepared when out-of-the-ordinary events are planned for the day (e.g., a field trip). Children with TBI who are in wheelchairs may need special assistance to get in and out of buses when wheelchair lifts are unavailable. If planning a field trip, check ahead of time if ramps are available for easy access by children in wheelchairs or those who wear braces.

- Children with traumatic brain injuries may need wheelchair lifts on the buses or vans they use for arrival and departure from schools or childcare centers. They also will need special assistance if they wear braces. Children attending public school typically are provided with transportation to and from school, and these vehicles usually are properly equipped. The physical environment should be evaluated to ensure that unnecessary barriers are removed that could cause a child in a wheelchair to tip over or struggle to move around.

- Teach children about safety drills (e.g., fire or tornado). Most children with TBI will be able to follow emergency procedures, but precautions are necessary if children are in wheelchairs or walk with a brace. Someone (most often you or an aide) should be responsible for assisting these children when responding to drills or actual emergencies and follow preset plans organized by schools or childcare centers. Children in wheelchairs may be required to exit their classrooms or schools by following alternate routes.

IF YOU WANT TO KNOW MORE

National Institute on Deafness and Other Communication Disorders
31 Center Drive, MSC 2320
Bethesda, MD 20892-2320
800-241-1044
http://nidcd.nih.gov

traumaticbraininjury.com
Ste. 1705, Two Penn Center Plaza
Philadelphia, PA 19102-1865
888-915-7600
http://www.traumaticbraininjury.com

Brain Injury Resource Center
P.O. Box 84151
Seattle, WA 98124-5451
206-621-8558
http://www.headinjury.com

National Resource Center for Traumatic Brain Injury
P.O. Box 980542
Richmond, VA 23298
804-828-9055
http://www.neuro.pmr.vcu.edu

National Dissemination Center for Children with Disabilities
1825 Connecticut Ave. NW, Ste. 700
Washington, DC 20009
800-695-0285
http://www.nichcy.org

CHAPTER 11

Adapting Classroom Materials to Meet the Needs of All Learners

SELECTING AND MAINTAINING CLASSROOM MATERIALS

As an early childhood educator, you are responsible for selecting and maintaining the materials in your classroom. As you plan lessons and organize classroom centers, you probably think of different ways to enhance children's learning. Creating an inclusive classroom often requires extra planning. Consideration of many factors is necessary in order to optimize the learning opportunities for all of the children in the group. Some factors to consider include the following.

Safety

Above all else, children must be safe when they are in the classroom. Are materials and paint lead-free? Do any toys or materials have small pieces that children might swallow, causing them to choke? Some sources suggest that phthalates, a component in plastics and some baby products, are dangerous to children's health. However, others indicate that safety reviews by European and American scientific panels have specifically cleared phthalates for use in toys and in nail polish (http://www.phthalates.org/whatare/index.asp). Consider checking with professional organizations and trusted Internet resources (such as those sponsored by governmental agencies) to find listings of toys that are inappropriate for young children.

Needs and Interests of Children

Toys must be attractive and appealing to children. Both teachers and families want toys that are interactive and that allow children to learn by using them. This reasoning supports the need for age-appropriate materials, which capture children's attention and capitalize on their natural curiosity about the world they live in. (See more about children's needs in the section below titled "Materials in Inclusion Classrooms.")

Instructional Value for Children

Katz and Chard (2000) suggested that children need materials that encourage them to think in novel and interesting ways. Matching children with materials and activities that are suitable and age-appropriate will promote their development from independent levels (children can use materials easily but may not be learning from them) to instructional levels (children are challenged to moderate achievement of skills and subskills for formal educational settings).

Your observation and diagnosis are imperative in determining if the match will help children learn skills required of them as they grow older and enter elementary school. The National Association for the Education of Young Children (NAEYC; Copple & Bredekamp, 2009) refers to teacher planning for individual children and groups as "developmentally appropriate practice" (p. 1).

MATERIALS IN INCLUSIVE CLASSROOMS

What is needed in the classroom to ensure the success of children with special needs? Generally, the response to this question is that children with special needs require accommodations and/or modifications in three primary areas: the classroom environment, the curriculum, and instruction (Warner et al., 2007). Specifically, children with special needs may require:

1. making alterations to the physical environment to increase participation,
2. modifying materials to promote independence,
3. using adaptive devices to facilitate participation, and
4. employing adult intervention and peer support.

Killoran and Brown (2006) suggested that modifications in the classroom environment, the curriculum, and instruction could possibly benefit children's typically developing peers in the inclusive classroom as well. They also suggested that teachers should collaborate with the early childhood special education intervention specialist to plan modifications and assess their success with individual children.

The experts with the Let's Play! Project (n.d.; a research model at the University of Buffalo in New York) recommended that toys and materials used with young children who have special needs take into account specific needs of each child (see http://www.letsplay.buffalo.edu/toys/special-toys.htm for more information). These include:

- stabilizing materials to prevent them from slipping (consider using Velcro®, carpet squares, suction cups, and grip liners);
- extending or building up materials for children (using modeling clay, craft sticks, foam padding, or other commercial materials);
- teaching children how to attach objects (using elastic straps, magic shoelaces, snaps, fabric tape, or commercial linking materials); and
- confining children's workspaces (using hula hoops, cookie sheets, or cardboard box tops).

In addition, the Let's Play! Project team has partnered with Fisher Price™ (see http://www.fisher-price.com/US/special_needs/default.asp for more information) to develop appropriate toys and materials for children with special needs. The Let's Play! Project has defined three stages of play as follows:

- experience stage ("What is this toy?"),
- discovery stage ("What does this toy do?"), and
- expanding imagination stage ("What else can I do with this toy?").

The Let's Play! Project (n.d.) team suggested that children with special needs need play experiences that will help them improve their functioning in these critical areas of development and learning, including:

- seeing,
- hearing,
- manipulating toys,
- thinking and learning,
- moving, and
- talking.

WHAT TEACHERS CAN DO FOR CHILDREN WITH SPECIAL NEEDS

Traditionally, programs for young children use the "centers approach" in preschool classrooms. For a sizable portion of the children's day, they play with their peers in established areas of the classroom that are prepared for children's learning. The most commonly used centers in early childhood classrooms are Blocks, Books, Home Living Center, Manipulatives and Puzzles (designed for fine motor development), Art Center, Writing Center, and the Dramatic Play Center. In addition, most large motor activity occurs during Outdoor Play. Some of the more useful adaptations and modifications for centers are:

- teacher intervention,
- peer-to-peer assistance,
- picture communication systems,
- directional posters and/or audiotapes,
- easy access to materials, and
- providing choices.

Teacher Intervention

The most important way for you to help children with special needs is to intervene when necessary. Carefully observe children as they interact with materials and their peers during their center activities. If a child becomes frustrated or has difficulty manipulating classroom materials, be prepared to step in to give the type of help a particular child needs. For example, if a child is in the Book Center and is having difficulty turning the pages in a book, offer to help him.

Peer-to-Peer Assistance

Children's typically developing peers also can be helpful in assisting children with special needs. If you promote a positive attitude toward children with special needs, most young children are eager to support those children who need help. They can learn how to guide a wheelchair into a center or they can help a child when he can't access a toy or object.

Picture Communication Systems

Children who are nonverbal or who have speech impairments can use picture communication to make requests or indicate their turn-taking preferences. Usually, these systems are teacher-made and can include small flash cards, posters, or wall charts. When developing your system, some helpful pictures to include are:

- bathrooms (child needs to use the bathroom);
- water fountains (child is thirsty);
- plates and cups (child is hungry);
- sleeping children (child is tired or sleepy);
- adults helping children (child needs assistance);
- children helping children (child wants assistance from other children); and
- pictures of emotional states (child can indicate his unhappiness, anger, frustration, pleasure, and so on in given situations).

Directional Posters and/or Audiotapes

Similar in nature to picture communication systems, directional posters and audiotapes are designed with instruction in mind. If, for example, you use a Cooking Center in the classroom, you might want to post a pictorial representation of each step in a recipe for children to follow. These adaptations are particularly helpful to children with hearing impairments. Audio versions of directions can be developed for children with vision impairments.

Easy Access to Materials

Whether children have special needs or not, it is important to provide easy access to toys and materials that children use regularly. Toys and materials should be kept at the children's level and children should be able to take them off the shelves or out of the cabinets with ease. This necessitates an understanding that children should have some level of control over their environment. This component of the classroom environment promotes independence. Again, your observation and intervention are critical to ensure that children with special needs have the same opportunities as all of the children in the classroom. For instance, if students generally stand to paint at easels, you may need to request adjustable easels so a child in a wheelchair can place his easel at his level or have all of the students sit on stools to paint.

Providing Choices

All children need opportunities to make choices about centers and materials they want to use. This choice process gives children a sense of empowerment. They learn perseverance when playing with what they have self-selected. Children with special needs experience the same feelings when they make choices about their activities, and the results for them are a sense of accomplishment and achievement. Making choices supports their social/emotional and cognitive needs and their desire to develop competency.

For additional information about adapting classroom materials, consider reading *The Inclusive Early Childhood Classroom: Easy Ways to Adapt Learning Centers for All Children* (Gould & Sullivan, 2005), *There's Room for Everyone: Accommodations, Supports, and Transitions—Infancy to Postsecondary* (Killoran & Brown, 2006), or "Adapting and Modifying Toys for Children With Special Needs" (ERIC Document #481092) by Cynthia Simpson and Sharon Lynch (2003). Another book, *Inclusive Lesson Plans Throughout the Year* by Laverne Warner, Sharon Lynch, Diana Nabors, and Cynthia Simpson (2007) described specific accommodations for lessons for preschoolers. *Themes for Inclusive Lesson Plans* (2008), by the same authors, also provided additional information on adapting and modifying lesson plans for the preschool classroom.

ACCOMMODATING AND MODIFYING
SPECIFIC CLASSROOM CENTERS

Table 6 will help you determine how to help children with special needs within specific classroom centers. This table provides options for modifying tools used in popular classroom centers, along with recommended toys for use in these centers.

OTHER ISSUES TO CONSIDER

Teachers in inclusive classrooms will always face challenges when making decisions for children with special needs. Other issues that often influence classroom learning and may impact your decision making are:

- the amount of space you have for organizing successful classrooms for diverse learners,
- how you organize and place the classroom centers in the room,
- the traffic flow in the classroom,
- whether volunteers and paraprofessionals are available for routine assistance in the classroom, and
- whether state or federal standards are expected of children and how you plan for instruction.

IF YOU WANT TO KNOW MORE

Toys for Special Needs Children
http://www.answers4families.org/family/special-needs/tools/toys-special-needs-children

Toys & Playtime Tips for Children With Special Needs
http://www.fisher-price.com/US/special_needs/default.asp

Let's Play!
http://www.letsplay.buffalo.edu/play/play.html

Play It Safe With Organic Toys
http://www.sumboshine.com/category_33/Organic_Toys.htm

Table 6

ADAPTATIONS OF TOYS FOR CLASSROOM CENTERS

Center	Adaptation	Recommended Toys
Block Center	• Use picture communication system (turn taking) • Build structures horizontally or vertically • Build structures against a wall • Use stabilization materials • Set boundaries with colored tape	• Bristle blocks • Legos® • Large cardboard blocks • Human figures • Cars • Trucks
Book Center	• Include audio recordings and headphones • Use storyboards that allow children to attach story props with Velcro® (include pictures showing environmental objects, such as fast food restaurant logos, popular snack foods, and so on)	• Cloth books • Picture books (for children to invent their own plots) • Books with large pictures and print • Puppets and puppet stage • Flannel board and story pieces
Home Living Center	• Make wide space for wheelchairs to enter • Have easy access to furniture in the center • Make realistic props (to the degree possible) • Have props that are easy to pick up and manipulate	• Diverse collection of dolls • Play telephone • Mirrors • Dress-up clothes • Realistic props that are found in the home (e.g., telephone books, magazines, newspapers)
Manipulatives/ Puzzles	• Make sure materials are easily stabilized • Provide materials that set boundaries (confinement) • If possible, consider water or sand tables with corresponding toys • Provide resealable bags for playdough • Use pipe cleaners for stringing beads	• Pegs and pegboards (if children are mature enough) • Clothespins • Puzzles with large pieces • Puzzles that have their own trays • Attribute blocks • Playdough • Wooden beads

Center	Adaptation	Recommended Toys
Art Center	• Build up handles on paintbrushes • Add grips to markers and crayons • Add scents or textures to prints • Tape art paper on easels • Outline figures with glue and sprinkle sand or glitter on the drawing • Use resealable plastic bags for playdough or other molding materials • Provide boundaries for art projects (e.g., box lids, cookie sheets)	• High-contrast colors of paint, crayons, and markers • Finger paints • Small scissors • Loop scissors • Paper for torn paper art • Straws for blowing paint • Sandpaper • Glue sticks • Easel (more than one, if possible)
Writing Center	• Allow children to stand when they use implements, if they choose • Build up handles on markers, crayons, and pencils • Use large pencils	• Variety of writing instruments • Variety of writing surfaces • Old greeting cards for children to cut and paste to make their own cards • Construction paper • Tissue paper • Scrap box for discarded paper
Dramatic Play Center	• Provide costumes that are easy to get into with Velcro® snaps • Take digital pictures of clothing as examples for children to emulate • Have a wide space for pretend play	• Variety of dress-up clothes • Props for pretend play • Shoes and purses • Costumes that represent current cultural figures (e.g., Spiderman)
Outdoor Play	• Add pedals with blocks and straps to wheeled toys and tricycles • Add Velcro® to balls and mitts • Enlarge targets • Provide swings with seatbacks	• Large and textured bags • Wagons • Beanbags • Scooter boards • Ball pit • Tunnel • Rocking horse

Note. Adapted from Simpson and Lynch (2003).

CHAPTER

12

Collaborating With Families of Children in Inclusive Classrooms

"I'm having my first parent/teacher conference tomorrow afternoon. Is there anything I need to know about planning and conducting the conference?" Ms. Davis asked as she entered Mrs. Shelton's classroom. Mrs. Shelton, a teacher with many years experience, quickly comprehended Ms. Davis' predicament—as a first-year teacher, she was apprehensive about having her first parent conference the following day.

"Who's the person coming to the conference?" Mrs. Shelton inquired.

"Thomas' mother and stepfather will be coming. I feel a little intimidated. What should I be prepared to tell them? What if they're unhappy with the way I teach?" Ms. Davis confided.

"I thought Thomas is one of the most well-behaved children in your class. Is he having problems learning?" Mrs. Shelton asked.

"He's well-behaved, and he gets along with others in the classroom. Am I worrying needlessly?" Ms. Davis replied.

Working with families is an acknowledged challenge that you will cope with whether you are new to the teaching profession or if you have taught for many years. In real-world teaching, connecting with families is not always easy to manage. Some parents or guardians are shy, some have difficulty understanding school expectations, others may have family problems (such as divorce or extreme work stress) that prevent healthy communication and, in some instances, language barriers may exist.

Forming a bond with children and their families requires skill to construct relationships that are positive, relevant, and meet the needs of the children that the school serves. Even greater obstacles emerge when working with children who have special needs. Creating a successful home/school connection requires patience, understanding, and an ability to develop an open-door policy that includes all families.

WHY IS THE HOME/SCHOOL CONNECTION IMPORTANT?

It is important to know and have insight into the lives of the families represented in your classroom. One of the five guidelines to developmentally appropriate practice the National Association for the Education of Young Children (Bredekamp & Copple, 1997) defined is "establishing reciprocal relationships with families" (p. 22). What this guideline recommends is that teachers and families collaborate to:

- share mutual respect for one another,
- maintain two-way communication in spontaneous interactions as well as scheduled conferences,
- work together to make decisions about the childcare and education program,
- understand one another's goals for children, and
- converse about children's activities in and out of school.

When collaboration exists, you will be able to:

- support families in finding services they need,
- work closely with individual children to ensure they have optimal educational opportunities,
- share developmental knowledge about children,
- ask for help from families in making decisions about children's needs, and
- invite parents or guardians to volunteer in a variety of ways in the classroom setting.

Collaboration supports families' confidence that their children are safe and protected at school. Families also become aware that their suggestions to the program's structure and content are welcome. As they gain an awareness that they are contributing to their child's education, they also begin to recognize the teacher as a caring person who is dedicated to achieving the best for their child (California Department of Education, 2000).

Turnbull et al. (2007) cited six important principles of family partnerships:

1. communication,
2. professional competence,
3. commitment,
4. equality,
5. advocacy, and
6. trust. (pp. 94–101)

The link among these principles is that you understand your role as a collaborator with the family for the benefit of the child (Yelland, 2000). The school's responsibility is to acknowledge the partnership and encourage families to make positive contributions to the early childhood program's success.

STRATEGIES FOR COMMUNICATING WITH FAMILIES

How can the early care and education community join forces with families and communities? Although the principles mentioned above are the answer to this question, the critical component to working with families is communication. Frequent and regular communication with families is at the heart of forming a healthy home/school relationship. What follows is a discussion of the specific strategies you can use to improve communication with the families you serve.

Conferences With Families

Ms. Davis' dilemma in the opening anecdote was one of concern that her first conference would go well. What is important to remember, no matter how many years of experience you have, is that families know their children. Because of your experience as a teacher, you have a perspective about children as it relates to the classroom. When conferences occur, both you and the families need to share your knowledge. Here are some specific tips for conducting successful conferences:

- Plan to talk for about 30 minutes and tell families about the time limit when they arrive.
- Close the classroom or conference room door to limit interruptions. Place a sign on the outside of the door that reads "Conference in Progress."
- Sit at a table near the family, not across from them. This strategy suggests that a partnership exists. Have samples of children's work available to show during the conference.
- Open the conference by asking the family to express any concerns they have. Although they may not respond to this request, you have opened the door for a conversation to develop as the conference progresses.
- If you have concerns about the child, choose one or two that families can address at home. Provide specific information they can use to improve their child's functioning. (See the next section for more about this tip.)
- Throughout the conference, try to remain relaxed and comfortable.
- Remember that the conference is a conversation about a specific child and the information learned in the discussion is confidential (Hendrick & Weissman, 2006).
- If you make promises to families during the conference, follow up as soon as possible. Make notes to yourself as soon as the conference ends, so that you will recall what you promised.

Although it is time-consuming to prepare for and conduct a conference, the benefits to children are twofold:

1. It gives you a greater understanding of children's behaviors and attitudes, and
2. it helps families become allies in the process of educating their children.

When you express concerns about individual children, families should leave the conference knowing how to help their children become more successful while they are in the classroom. For example, say that one of the children does not know her home address, which is a skill children learn in preschool. You can say, "We've been working on learning our home addresses, and Nora doesn't appear to know hers yet. Would you be willing to review your address at home?" If the family member asks how to teach this information, respond with several suggestions, such as:

- Repeat it with her several times during the week.
- Show the number to her on the outside of your home or apartment.
- If the child has shown an interest in writing, show her what the address looks like by printing it on a piece of paper for her.
- Share an envelope with her that has the address on it.
- Emphasize the reasons why people need to know their address.

Remember to limit your problems or concerns to one or two issues that are manageable by families. For inexperienced teachers, the temptation is to define every problem that the child needs to work on. This could overwhelm families and they may leave the conference feeling that there is no hope for their child. In a sense, you destroy the trust with families that you are trying to develop. Help families feel a sense of empowerment in their relationship with you as their child's teacher.

Communicating Effectively

Becoming an effective communicator implies that you become a better listener and responder to family concerns. Having knowledge of and utilizing specific skills that will improve communication opportunities will maximize your discussions with families about their children. Warner and Sower (2005) defined these skills as:

- Establishing and maintaining eye contact as you listen to families.
- Developing a positive relationship with families prior to being completely open about the concerns you have for their child.
- Understanding the emotional ability of the family, whether they can handle the child's situation or not, and adjusting your discussion with them accordingly.
- Clarifying what families have said about their children and providing concrete suggestions for solving the problem they address (or recommending community resources for them).

- Using language that families will understand when having conferences or informative discussions with them about their children (avoid educational jargon).
- Refraining from placing blame on families for children's difficulties.
- Being enthusiastic about children's achievements and acknowledging the family's role in helping their child to be successful. (p. 406)

Newsletters

The parent-teacher conference is not the only approach to communicating with families. Most schools and centers use a traditional communication method with families—newsletters. Newsletters are useful because they allow you to share timely information about upcoming events or convey child development knowledge that families need to know about their children. Newsletters can be one page or many pages, depending on your (or the school's) expertise and goal for the newsletter.

Some schools and centers develop campuswide newsletters that go home with every child, while others expect teachers to plan and transmit newsletters for their classroom clientele. Either way, newsletters represent a tool that encourages families to become participants in the life of the school. Items that can be included in newsletters are:

- content about what children are learning while they are in school (e.g., themes, special lessons, skills developed, educational classroom activities, classroom responsibilities);
- songs, fingerplays, chants, and rhymes that children are learning;
- dates for special events (e.g., class photographs, field trips, special visitors, scheduled programs, class celebrations);
- weekly menus or monthly schedules;
- information about scheduled screenings (e.g., vision, hearing, dental);
- reminders about forms that families need to return to the school (e.g., field trip permissions, insurance forms, vaccination verification);
- requests for family involvement (e.g., chaperones for field trip visits, volunteers for parties, field days, book sharing, art projects, fundraising activities);

- requests for family members to come to school to share information about topics of study (e.g., people who work in various professions and careers, such as firefighters, police officers, and dentists), musicians, and other individuals who have unique skills (e.g., someone who can perform stunts, juggle, or do magic tricks);
- timely information about contagious diseases that are prevalent in the community (e.g., pink eye);
- child development information that families might need to understand their children's social and emotional needs (or links to Web sites that provide family support); and
- anecdotal information about activities and projects children are doing in the classroom (digital cameras might be used to document some of this classroom experience).

One tip to remember is to send letters home to families using the language they know. You may need to consider hiring a translator to write letters and notes in the child's home language. A sample newsletter is available in Figure 6 to guide readers in preparing their own efforts.

Notes Home

One quick and easy way to communicate with the family is to send a note home at the end of the day. Jotting a message to families takes little time, and may be just the right approach for connecting to the home. Notes should be short and to the point, and written in the language the family uses at home. To maintain professional competence (Turnbull et al., 2007), read the note at least two times before sending it home (or have a colleague proof your writing).

Telling families that Cameron "counted to 10 today" or "demonstrated good behavior on the playground" is a way to follow-up with concerns expressed in a family conference without having to schedule another one when time is tight for you and families. Noting that "Alicia appears to be getting ill" will alert a family member to a possibility that someone will have to stay home to take care of Alicia or find other suitable care for her the next day.

Angie's Preschool

March 16

Dear Families:

Hasn't the rain been great this week? The staff and the children here at Angie's Preschool are ready for some sunny weather, and it appears that the upcoming weekend will be great.

I wanted to remind you of the Walker County Fair and Rodeo scheduled for March 31 through April 7. Many of you have children who will be showing their animals, and I am aware that at least two of our parents are entering jams and cakes in the food contests.

Remember, too, that we will be taking all of the 4- and 5-year-olds to the fair's Preschool Day, planned for Wednesday, April 4.

We'll need a few volunteers to help with this trip, so call me if you are available (234-5555). We plan to leave the center at 9 and return by 11 a.m. Hope you can join us!

Also, a reminder to you that the field trip permission slips should be returned by Friday, March 30, if your child is able to attend. You'll find another one on the back of this newsletter if you've misplaced the one we sent to you earlier in the month.

As always, we at Angie's Preschool are enjoying your children. You're always welcome to visit us and watch them learn.

Sincerely,
Angie Sherman
Owner & Director

Weekly Lunch Menu

Monday—Turkey Chili

Tuesday—Ravioli

Wednesday—Burgers

Thursday—Pizza Rolls

Friday—Corn Dogs

One of the Songs We've Been Learning This Week
Tune: "My Bonnie Lies Over the Ocean" (verse only)

St. Patrick's Day is here;
this day is fun, it's clear!
I'll put on some clothes
that are green
And pretend I am
Irish, my dear!

April Calendar of Events

Friday, April 6—We will be open for business as usual (public schools will not)

Tuesday, April 10—Picture Day (ask your child's teacher about the times scheduled for her classroom)

Thursday, April 19— Parent Potluck Speaker from Families Supporting Families— Topic: "Understanding Children With Special Needs and Abilities"

Friday, April 27— Enrollment forms for the 2007–2008 year are due.

Field Trip Permission Form

My child (please insert his or her name) _____
may attend the Walker County Fair Preschool Day scheduled on Wednesday, April 4.

Signature of Parent or Guardian_____

Please return to your child's teacher by Friday, March 30.

FIGURE 6. Sample newsletter.

Parent Handbooks

Many schools and centers develop family handbooks and give them to families when children enroll. These booklets provide vital information about policies and procedures that guide the relationship that professionals and families develop. School personnel usually develop these handbooks, but occasionally families share a responsibility in the process. Policies and procedures might include:

- philosophical orientation toward children's development and learning,
- information about the guidance system used in the school,
- what happens when children become ill at school,
- procedures for keeping children home when they are sick,
- what happens when an accident occurs,
- information about the curriculum used in the school,
- what children are expected to learn during the year,
- policies about religious holidays and celebrations,
- procedures for collection of enrollment payments (especially in childcare centers),
- safety procedures used in the school or center,
- grievance procedures, and
- other information that the school or center deems is essential to positive school/home connections.

Routinely reviewing handbooks and adding policies as necessary are essential tools to provide the most up-to-date information for families about what goes on at school. Handbooks, like most public documents, are works in progress.

Spontaneous Conversations

Schools and centers located in smaller communities (50,000 or fewer people) will provide opportunities for families and teachers to meet in many locations—grocery stores, post offices, ballparks, churches or synagogues, public events, libraries—almost anywhere in the community. These contacts provide unique opportunities to interact positively and strengthen the home/school bond.

The key when having a spontaneous conversation is to refrain from confronting families with comments that are more appropriate to share in private conferences. Confidentiality is of the essence for all families, so keep discussion in these brief encounters cordial, positive, and encouraging. Mentioning something that the child did at school on that day (or during the week) is appropriate. Inviting families to set up an appointment for a conference may be critical, but going into detail about the nature of the conference is not.

Brochures and Articles

Sharing child development information and insight into the curriculum at your school is another way to connect with families. If you find a timely article in a professional journal that meets the needs of your students, check the copyright permission policy in the journal to learn if you can make copies of the article to send home to families. The National Association for the Education of Young Children (NAEYC) states that no permission is necessary to make copies from *Young Children* and *Teaching Young Children* as long as users distribute the articles at no cost and that NAEYC receives credit, so these sources are ideal for sharing information.

NAEYC also has information for families on its Web site that can be shared with parents (http://www.naeyc.org). The "For Families" section on the NAEYC home page provides an "Early Years Are Learning Years" component with articles of interest for parents to read, such as "Helping Toddlers Become Problem Solvers" or "Helping Young Children Start School."

The Web site also offers books for purchase as well as brochures, which are available for bulk purchase for distribution in schools and childcare centers. A few of the brochures are "Play Is FUNdamental," "Keeping Healthy: Families, Teachers, and Children," and "Helping Children Learn Self-Control: A Guide to Discipline." Schools and childcare centers can order these brochures and have them available for parent pickup in a common area, such as the front office or school lobby.

The Southern Early Childhood Association (SECA; http://www.southernearlychildhood.org) offers Parent Pages to download (for members only) and includes Spanish versions as well. Another resource is a listserv, exchangeeveryday@ccie.com, that disseminates daily articles for childcare providers. The topics range from information about brain development to the importance of art experiences in preschool to overcoming cultural biases. Some of the articles would be excellent resources for families. If you have your families listed on an e-mail listserv connection, you could forward appropriate articles to them as they appear.

For specific information regarding disability awareness, federal legislation, advocacy efforts, and teacher resources, you can visit the Council for Exceptional Children Web site at http://www.cec.sped.org. For other informative sources, please see the Annotated Web Resources in Appendix C.

Telephone Calls

Ensuring that your families' phone number(s) are included in your records as children enroll almost seems unnecessary to mention, because we rely on telephone communications every day. Remembering to include alternative phone numbers (e.g., work phone numbers, cell phone numbers, numbers for the nearest relative, neighbors' phone numbers) is all part of the data we collect when children first come to school.

Telephone calls to families can enhance any relationship when you make them for any of the following reasons:

- a courtesy call before the child comes to school for the first time to introduce yourself to the family;
- just to tell the family something the child did that day that was significant (able to recognize her name for the first time or name all of the color words);
- as a follow-up to a concern that emerged during a family conference;
- a reminder to come to a special event scheduled after hours at the school;
- to communicate a special congratulations to the family (e.g., if they are going on a special trip or having a baby); and
- as a thank you for contributions the family may have made to the school (e.g., volunteer hours or doing something special with the children).

Sometimes phone calls to the home may need to convey a concern you have (such as regarding children's progress in school or misbehavior that has emerged), but using the phone call to communicate positive messages goes a long way in enhancing the relationship and collaboration you want to develop with families. Use conferences to communicate concerns about children's educational progress, because face-to-face interaction is much more effective for these messages.

Electronic Transmissions

Using e-mail and instant messaging does depend on the availability of computers in the home (or work) and at school, as well as Internet capabilities in both places. In the current age of technology, electronic connections often are the fastest way to communicate with some families. As the year progresses, you will discover which families rely on their computers for contacts about their children and which do not. Adjust your electronic transmissions as you determine the extent to which they are effective.

INVOLVING FAMILIES IN THE LIFE OF THE SCHOOL OR CENTER

The overall goal of home/school connections is to help families understand their role in the education of their children. Helping families connect with the school implies that they must become involved in the goings-on of the childcare center, the school, or other public entity. The school's attempts to include families in school activities sets an "open door" atmosphere that encourages parents to become interested in what and how their children are learning (Warner & Sower, 2005). These opportunities for involvement provide cognitive growth, language development, and social development in children. The following are descriptions of some of the more common approaches to parental involvement.

Open Houses

In the beginning of the year, schools and centers schedule an open house and invite families to come see their children's classroom and meet their child's teachers. Usually, families bring their children, and individual children are able to show their families what they like about their classrooms and talk about the activities they do during the day. Teachers may take a few minutes to talk to the families as a group telling some of their goals for the school year or reminding families of some of the school's policies.

This time is for you and your students' families to make your first acquaintances with one another. When families want to talk about their child, asking questions that they prefer to remain confidential, ask them to make an appointment for a conference. You may need to explain, "I like to keep information about all of the children confidential. This is not a good time for me to answer that question. When can we set up a conference?"

Special Programs

Children enjoy celebrations, and special programs allow these to happen. Monthly potluck suppers or spring picnics provide families with reasons for being involved with the school. Children can sing songs, recite poems, or conduct simple dramatic reenactments to add to the festive nature of any social outing. Again, these events are not an appropriate venue for discussing children, but they are important venues for helping families understand the role and function of the school. Also consider calling upon families to help plan and implement a special program, thus providing another approach to parental involvement. Organized field days or end-of-the-year celebrations supply family memories for a lifetime!

Volunteerism

Numerous occasions require family volunteers during the school year. Asking families as they enroll their children to identify areas where they are willing to volunteer is an effective approach to getting the information you need from them. You also can send out requests for volunteers in regular newsletters or e-mail transmissions. Remember to ask fathers and other male family members for assistance to ensure involvement throughout the family. Some volunteer activities include:

- ◆ reading books to small groups of children (or individually);

- assisting one or two children with designated skills (e.g., learning to put puzzles together or counting);
- serving as music teacher on a routine basis (especially if your school cannot afford one);
- setting up displays of artifacts for children to play with (ask parents not to include anything fragile or valuable);
- accompanying children on field trips;
- cutting out letters or figures for bulletin boards;
- making costumes for the Dress-Up Center;
- serving as a clerical assistant for collecting and putting children's favorite recipes into a booklet as a fundraising project;
- asking families to donate items for classroom use;
- building a new fence for the playground;
- having a paint-and-repair day for the school; and
- other ideas that support educational experiences for children.

Advisory Boards

Family members can be invaluable on school advisory boards. Usually advisory boards meet on a quarterly basis during the year and discuss information as it relates to school operations. Family input to the development of yearly calendars, review of policies and procedures, how to involve all families, and problems families perceive relating to school functions allows trust to develop between the home and school (Turnbull et al., 2007). You and school administrators benefit when families begin to understand why specific policies and procedures exist. True collaboration evolves when schools respect what families have to offer and families recognize their impact on school operations.

HELPING FAMILIES UNDERSTAND THE INCLUSIVE CLASSROOM

One aspect of an inclusive classroom is creating a sense of community within the environment. In establishing community, all families (including those with children with special needs and those with typically developing children) need to feel welcome and encouraged to ask questions regarding their child's placement in the classroom. It is a myth to believe that only those families whose children do not have special needs will question the value of an inclusive setting. In actuality, any family may raise concerns about the safety and the amount of progress that their child will experience.

In helping families to understand the inclusive classroom, try to remain open and honest about the outcomes and challenges children will experience. Most teachers find it helpful to explain to parents the benefits for all involved in the classroom, paying particular attention to the benefits for children with special needs, children who are typically developing, families of children with special needs, families of typically developing children, and the community. Wolery and Wilbers (1994) provided an excellent framework for discussing benefits of inclusion with families.

Children who are typically developing also benefit from the inclusive setting by being around children who successfully accomplish goals despite their special needs. In addition, children develop friendships with children with special needs and learn firsthand about the characteristics of specific disabilities. Families of both children with and without disabilities gain the opportunity to teach their children about how each person has his or her own set of strengths and that each person is different. This understanding at a young age will directly impact the success rate of inclusion in elementary and middle school and, eventually, assist children in their acceptance of differences throughout their lives.

As with any good early learning program, family communication is essential. In an inclusive classroom, this is particularly true. Often in an inclusive classroom, particular events may occur that the children may or may not have experienced before. For example, in a classroom for 4-year-olds, a child with a severe disability may still be wearing diapers and learning to use the toilet. Children may come home and ask their families why Mary Ann is wearing diapers. If open lines of communication are established, families can support your efforts by explaining the issue to their children. Although it is necessary to maintain a level of confidentiality, you should encourage communication between all families at open house, special events, and family meetings.

By breaking down the specific benefits for everyone involved, families can clearly see why inclusive classrooms are the ideal learning environment for their children. Some of the benefits that an inclusive classroom offers for children with special needs are providing peer role models, opportunities for children with disabilities to be exposed to proper modeling of language and behaviors, and the opportunity to eliminate negative attitudes contributed to by isolation and labeling.

Glossary of Terms

As teachers and administrators work with children who have special needs, their understanding of special education terminology is important as they interact with parents, colleagues and special education professionals. The following terms and their definitions, adapted and revised in part from *Inclusive Lesson Plans Throughout the Year* by Laverne Warner, Sharon Lynch, Diana Nabors, and Cynthia Simpson (2007), are meant to facilitate a dialogue among those concerned about children in their classrooms.

Accommodations: Changing instruction to provide an appropriate way for children with disabilities to access information and demonstrate mastery of skills.

Aphasia: An inability to produce or to comprehend language.

Audiologist: A professional trained in diagnosing, treating, and managing individuals with hearing loss and balance disorders.

ASL: American Sign Language.

Assistive technology: Any device or software that can maximize a person's potential or increase his or her abilities to acquire skills.

Attention Deficit/Hyperactivity Disorder: Children with serious problems with overactivity, attention, or both.

Autism: Children who typically have difficulty in communication and social interactions.

Cognitive and/or developmental delays: Children who have slower-than-normal development and mental functioning.

Conductive hearing loss: Hearing loss that is most common. It usually can be treated through medication or surgery. This type of loss often is associated with impacted earwax, fluid on the ear, allergies, and/or infection.

Developmentally appropriate practices (DAP) : An orientation toward teaching children that considers their age, individual abilities, needs and interests, and culture when determining what classroom activities should be used with them (often referred to as "best practices"); these practices are defined by professional organizations such as the Division for Early Childhood (DEC) of the Council for Exceptional Children (CEC) and the National Association for the Education of Young Children (NAEYC).

DSM-IV manual: A reference that is published by the American Psychiatric Association and used by psychologists, psychiatrists, and physicians when seeking information regarding diagnoses and treatment options for numerous disorders.

Echolalia: This is when a child repeats words and phrases that are spoken, either immediately after they are spoken or at a later time.

FM system: An amplification system worn around the neck of child with a hearing impairment. The teacher wears a microphone that broadcasts to the child's FM receiver.

Hand-over-hand assistance: The placement of the teacher's hands directly over a child's hands as he or she assists the child with a specific task.

Hearing impairment: A loss of hearing that causes speech and language delay, which may lead to learning problems, social isolation, and poor self-concept.

High-tech assistive technology devices: Devices that are commercially produced, sometimes expensive, and include a wide variety of equipment from Braille note takers, power wheelchairs (for children with orthopedic impairments or multiple disabilities), FM systems, software programs, and computers with high-tech devices such as voice-activated word processors, screen magnifiers, and alternative keyboards.

IEP: An Individualized Education Program is an educational plan for children's education from ages 3–21 when they meet the eligibility criteria to receive special education services.

IFSP: An Individualized Family Service Plan is an individualized written plan that is designed for families of children with disabilities to follow during the birth to age 3 intervention process. Some of the information identified in the IFSP includes related services, family support services, and nutrition services, as well as case management information.

Impulsive behaviors: Specific behaviors that occur without direct intention or thought from the child and often are difficult for a child to control.

Inattentive child: A child who is inattentive, often gets bored with something he or she is doing, is distracted easily, has problems following directions, and forgets to write things down (often seen in older children).

Inclusion classrooms: Classrooms that include all children, both with and without disabilities.

Individualized assessment: A requirement of the Americans with Disabilities Act that requires early childhood settings to assess children to determine if their program can meet the needs of the individual child; childcare centers are expected to make reasonable modifications to accommodate the child in question.

Language impairment: An impairment that directly interferes with a child's ability to understand language (receptive), or to speak what one intends to say (expressive), or both.

Lap pad: Term used to define a weighted pad, such as a bean-filled stocking, that is placed on a child's lap to remind him or her to remain seated.

Learned helplessness: Children who have continuous failures in mental or physical functioning learn to be helpless so others will perform activities they are capable of doing themselves.

Least restrictive environment (LRE): An environment that allows children with disabilities to be educated with normally functioning children.

Low-tech assistive technology devices: Devices that usually are simple, inexpensive, and often homemade, including pencil grips, large paper clips used to help children turn pages (if they have small motor problems), and simple switches that allow children to activate classroom toys.

Mixed hearing loss: Occurs when a child has a combination of sensorineural and conductive loss.

Modifications: Necessary changes to expected criteria on assessment activities for children with disabilities.

Natural environments: Usually refers to a child's home, but also can mean a community environment such as a childcare setting; any setting where an age-equivalent nondisabled peer might be functioning.

Object cues: An object, such as a toy or household material, predetermined by the child and teacher, that is used as a prompt to elicit a response from a child.

Occupational therapist: A professional who works primarily with assisting the child with sensory issues and fine motor deficits.

Orthopedic impairment: A physical disability, or motor difficulty, that may be caused by disease (e.g., poliomyelitis, bone tuberculosis) or impairments from other causes (e.g., cerebral palsy, amputations, fractures or burns that cause contractures).

Paraprofessional (or paraeducator): An adult in the classroom who assists children with tasks they are unable to perform on their own.

Peer assistant or peer buddy: Assigning one child to another to assist on a regular basis as needed or to help complete a specified task or activity.

Peer modeling: Requesting some children to demonstrate acceptable or appropriate behaviors to other children in the room.

Physical therapist: A professional who focuses on large motor issues, providing information about improving the child's large motor development.

Picture communication system: An alternative communication system composed of icons or pictures to assist a child in communicating his or her wants or needs.

Picture cues: Photograph or picture representations that elicit responses from a child.

Picture schedule: A representation of the daily schedule through icons or photographs displayed in the classroom.

Preschool inclusion models: Prototypes of assistance to the early childhood community that have evolved as a requirement of the Early Intervention Program for Infants and Toddlers with Disabilities.

Preteach: Teaching a specific skill or concept to a child prior to the time when the skill or concept is formally introduced to the class.

Proximity control: Placing the child within a certain distance from the teacher so the teacher is close enough to intervene as necessary. This distance serves as a reminder to the child of the teacher's presence to help the child maintain appropriate behaviors.

Receptive language impairment: Focuses on a child's ability to understand, not speak, the language.

Reinforcement: Use of extrinsic or intrinsic means, such as verbal praise or stickers, to encourage a behavior to occur again.

Scaffold: Method in which someone with more knowledge helps a person with limited knowledge understand a given concept or response by providing a series of cues in order to ensure a correct response.

Self-stimulation: Repetitive behavior that causes sensory gratification (sometimes called "stimming").

Sensorineural hearing loss: A hearing loss that cannot be treated by medications or surgery and indicates that damage is done to the inner ear or nerve passages to the inner ear. This is a form of permanent hearing loss.

Sensory defensiveness: Defines children's responses to their environment; some children are highly sensitive to tactile experiences (touch) while others are sensitive to movement and sound.

Sequence activities: Instruction that helps a child to understand the concept of putting objects or events in order.

Speech and language impairment: When children have problems with receptive and expressive language.

Speech-language pathologist: A professional who diagnoses and treats speech and language development problems.

Tactile defensiveness: Children with an inability to tolerate touch either due to over- or underreactivity to sensation.

Transition cues: Any form of cueing (e.g., verbal, object, or visual) to prepare a child to move from one activity to another.

Verbal cue: A spoken prompt that elicits a response from a child.

Vision impairment: Children who experience limited vision that adversely affects their educational experience.

Visual or physical cue: An easily identified symbol or physical object that visually prompts a child to respond.

Visual proximity: Keeping a child within the visual range of the teacher.

Wait time: The amount of time given to a child for a response. Ample wait time would be based on the child's cognitive ability to plan and make a response.

References

American Association on Intellectual and Developmental Disabilities. (2009). *Definition of intellectual disability.* Retrieved from http://www.aaidd.org/content_100.cfm?navID=21

American Printing House for the Blind. (2005). *Distribution of federal quota.* Retrieved from http://www.aph.org

American Psychiatric Association. (2000). *Diagnostic and statistical manual of mental disorders, Text revision* (4th ed.). Washington, DC: American Psychiatric Association.

American Speech-Language-Hearing Association. (1982). Committee on Language, Speech and Hearing Services in Schools: Definitions of communicative disorders and variations. *ASHA, 24,* 949–950.

American Speech-Language-Hearing Association. (2007). *Effects of hearing loss on development.* Retrieved from http://www.asha.org/public/hearing/disorders/effects.htm

Americans with Disabilities Act, 42 U.S.C. §§ 12102 et seq. (1990).

Assistive Technology Act of 1998, 29 U. S. C. §3001 et seq.

Bennett, R. (1995). *Friends at school.* Long Island City, NY: Star Bright Books.

Biederman, J., Faraone, S. V., Keenan, K., Knee, D., & Tsuang, M. T. (1990). Family-genetic and psychosocial risk factors in DSM-III attention deficit disorder. *Journal of the American Academy of Child & Adolescent Psychiatry, 29,* 526–533.

Biederman, J., Faraone, S. V., Mick, E., Spencer, T., Wilens, T., Kiely, K., et al. (1995). High-risk for Attention Deficit Hyperactivity Disorder among children of parents with childhood onset of the disorder: A pilot study. *American Journal of Psychiatry, 152,* 431–435.

Bredekamp, S., & Copple, C. (Eds.). (1997). *Developmentally appropriate practice in early childhood programs* (Rev. ed.). Washington, DC: National Association for the Education of Young Children.

California Department of Education. (2000). *Prekindergarten learning & development guidelines.* Sacramento: California Department of Education. Retrieved from http://www.cde.ca.gov/sp/cd/re/prekguide.asp

Cohen, M. (2009). *Will I have a friend?* Long Island City, NY: Star Bright Books.

Coleman, C., Yaruss, J. S., & Hammer, D. (2004). Parent/child treatment for preschool children who stutter. In A. Packmann, A. Meltzer, & H. F. M. Peters (Eds.), *Theory, research, and therapy in fluency disorders: Proceedings of the Fourth World Congress on Fluency Disorders* (pp. 117–122). Nijmegen, The Netherlands: Nijmegen University Press.

Cook, R., Klein, M., & Tessier, A. (2008). *Adapting early childhood curricula for children with special needs* (7th ed.). Upper Saddle River, NJ: Pearson.

Copple, C., & Bredekamp, S. (Eds.). (2009). *Developmentally appropriate practice in early childhood programs serving children from birth through age 8* (3rd ed.). Washington, DC: National Association for the Education of Young Children.

Division for Early Childhood. (2005). *Developmental delay as an eligibility category.* Missoula, MT: Author.

Division for Early Childhood, & National Association for the Education of Young Children. (2009). *Early childhood inclusion: A joint position statement of the Division for Early Childhood (DEC) and the National Association for the Education of Young Children (NAEYC).* Chapel Hill: The University of North Carolina, FPG Child Development Institute.

Dunlap, L. (2008). *An introduction to early childhood special education, birth to age five.* Upper Saddle River, NJ; Pearson.

Dunn, L., & Dunn, L. (1997). *Peabody Picture Vocabulary Test III.* Circle Pines, MN: American Guidance Service.

Education for All Handicapped Children Act of 1975, Pub. Law 94-142 (November 29, 1975).

Elementary and Secondary Education Act of 1965, §142, 20 U.S.C. 863.

Feit, D. (2007). *The parent's guide to speech and language problems.* New York: McGraw Hill.

Gould, P., & Sullivan, J. (2005). *The inclusive early childhood classroom: Easy ways to adapt learning centers for all children.* Upper Saddle River, NJ: Pearson.

Gray, C. (1991). *Social stories.* Retrieved from http://www.thegraycenter.org

Hamaguchi, P. (2001). *Childhood speech, language and listening problems: What every parent should know.* New York: Wiley.

Hendrick, D. L., Prather, E. M., & Tobin, A. R. (1984). *Sequenced inventory of communicative development.* Seattle: University of Washington Press.

Hendrick, J., & Weissman, P. (2006). *The whole child* (8th ed.). Upper Saddle River, NJ: Pearson.

Hodson, B. W. (1986). *Assessment of phonological processes, revised.* Austin, TX: Pro-Ed.

Honos-Webb, L. (2005). *The gift of ADHD: How to transform your child's problems into strengths.* Oakland, CA: Harbinger Publications.

Hooper, S., & Umansky, W. (2009). *Young children with special needs* (5th ed.). Upper Saddle River: Pearson.

Huecker, G., & Kinnealey, M. (1998). Prevalence of sensory integrative disorders in children with attention deficit hyperactivity disorder: A descriptive study. *The Journal of Developmental and Learning Disabilities, 2,* 265–292.

Individuals with Disabilities Education Act, 20 U.S.C. §1401 et seq. (1990).

Individuals with Disabilities Education Act, PL 105-17, 111 Stat. 37 (1997).

Individuals with Disabilities Education Improvement Act, PL 108-446, 118 Stat. 2647 (2004).

Isbell, C., & Isbell, R. (2007). *Sensory integration: A guide for preschool teachers.* Beltsville, MD: Gryphon House.

Katz, L., & Chard, S. (2000). *Engaging children's minds: The project approach* (2nd ed.). Stamford, CT: Ablex Publishing Corporation.

Keating, D., Ozanne, A., & Turrell, G. (2005). Childhood speech disorders: Reported prevalence, comorbidity and socioeconomic profile. *Journal of Pediatrics and Child Health, 37,* 431–436.

Killoran, I., & Brown, M. (Eds.). (2006). *There's room for everyone: Accommodations, supports, and transitions—Infancy to postsecondary.* Olney, MD: Association for Childhood Education International.

Lawlis, F. (2005). *The ADD answer.* New York: Plume.

Let's Play! Project. (n.d.). *Selecting toys.* Retrieved July 29, 2009, from http://www.letsplay.buffalo.edu/toys/toys.htm

Lightsey, R. L. (1993). Tactile defensiveness in attention deficit/hyperactive disorder children. *Sensory Integration Quarterly, 21*(2), 6.

Lynch, S. A. (2009). Understanding recommendations for identification and programming. In V. G. Spencer & C. G. Simpson (Eds.), *Teaching children with autism in the general classroom* (pp. 5–27). Waco, TX: Prufrock Press.

Lynch, S. A., & Simpson, C. G. (2007). Social stories: A new way to teach positive behaviors. *Early Years, Journal of the Texas Association for the Education of Young Children, 29*(3), 16–19.

Mastropieri, M., & Scruggs, T. (2004). *The inclusive classroom: Strategies for effective instruction* (2nd ed.). Upper Saddle River, NJ: Pearson.

Mastropieri, M., & Scruggs, T. (2007). Teaching students with higher-incidence disabilities. In *The inclusive classroom: Strategies for effective instruction* (3rd ed., pp. 52–54). Upper Saddle River, NJ: Pearson.

Mastropieri, M., & Scruggs, T. (2010). *The inclusive classroom: Strategies for effective differentiated instruction* (4th ed.). Upper Saddle River, NJ: Pearson.

MayoClinic.com. (2006). *Traumatic brain injury.* Retrieved from http://www.mayoclinic.com/health/traumatic-brain-injury/DS00552

Murray, C. G. (2007). *Simple signing with young children: A guide for infant, toddler, and preschool teachers.* Beltsville, MD: Gryphon House.

National Dissemination Center for Children with Disabilities. (2004). *Visual impairments* (Fact Sheet 13). Retrieved from http://www.nichcy.org/pubs/factshe/fs13txt.htm

National Institute of Mental Health. (2006). *Attention deficit hyperactivity disorder*. Bethesda, MD: Author. Retrieved from http://www.nimh.nih.gov/health/publications/adhd/summary.shtml

Odom, S. L., Horn, E. M., Marquart, J., Hanson, M. J., Wolfberg, P., Beckman, P., et al. (1999). On the forms of inclusion: Organizational context and service delivery models. *Journal of Early Intervention, 22*, 185–199.

Overton, T. (2008). *Assessing learners with special needs: An applied approach* (6th ed.). Upper Saddle River, NJ: Prentice Hall.

Parush, S. H., Sohmer, A., Steinberg, A., & Kaitz, M. (2007). Somatosensory function in boys with ADHD and tactile defensiveness. *Physiology & Behavior, 90*, 553–558.

Pfiffner, L. J. (1996). *All about ADHD: The complete practical guide for classroom teachers*. Jefferson City, MO: Scholastic.

Rafferty, Y. (2002). *Creating high quality inclusion programs for preschoolers with disabilities in New York City: A guide for preschool providers*. Retrieved from http://www.advocatesforchildren.org/pubs/PreSchoolFinal.pdf

Raver, S. (2009). *Early childhood special education—0 to 8 years, strategies for positive outcomes*. Upper Saddle River, NJ: Pearson.

Rogers, F. (1996). *Making friends*. New York: Putnam.

Rutledge, R. (2008). *When your child has ADD/ADHD*. Avon, MA: Adams Media.

Section 504 of the Rehabilitation Act, 29 U.S.C. Section 706 et. Seq. (1973).

Simpson, C., & Lynch, S. (2003). *Adapting and modifying toys for children with special needs*. Huntsville, TX: Sam Houston State University. (ERIC Document Reproduction Service No. ED481092)

Smith, B., & Rapport, M. J. (1999). *IDEA and early childhood inclusion*. Denver: The Collaborative Planning Project, University of Colorado.

Spencer, V., & Simpson, C. (2009). *Teaching children with autism in the general classroom*. Waco, TX: Prufrock Press.

Spencer, V., Simpson, C., & Lynch, S. (2008). Using social stories to increase positive behaviors for children with autism spectrum disorder. *Intervention School and Clinic, 44*, 58–61.

Taylor, R., Smiley, L., & Richards, S. (2008). *Exceptional students: Preparing teachers for the 21st century*. Boston, MA: McGraw Hill.

Turnbull, A., Turnbull, R., & Wehmeyer, M. (2007). *Exceptional lives: Special education in today's schools* (5th ed.). Upper Saddle River, NJ: Pearson.

Warner, L., & Lynch, S. (2004). *Preschool classroom management*. Beltsville, MD: Gryphon House.

Warner, L., Lynch, S., Nabors, D., & Simpson, C. G. (2007). *Inclusive lesson plans throughout the year*. Beltsville, MD: Gryphon House.

Warner, L., Lynch, S., Nabors, D., & Simpson, C. G. (2008). *Themes for inclusive lesson plans*. Beltsville, MD: Gryphon House.

Warner, L., & Sower, J. (2005). *Educating young children from preschool through primary grades*. Boston: Pearson.

Wehmeyer, M., Sands, S., Knowlton, D., & Kozleski, E. (2002). *Teaching students with mental retardation: Providing access to the general curriculum*. Baltimore: Brookes.

Weinfeld, R., & Davis, M. (2008). *Special needs advocacy resource book*. Waco, TX: Prufrock Press.

Wig, E. H., Semel, E. M., & Secord, W. A. (2004). *Clinical evaluation of language fundamentals—Preschool (CELF-P)*. San Antonio, TX: Harcourt/Psychological.

Willis, C. (2006). *Teaching young children with autism spectrum disorder*. Beltsville, MD: Gryphon House.

Winter, S. (2007). *Inclusive early childhood education: A collaborative approach*. Boston: Pearson.

Wolery, R. A., & Odom, S. L. (2000). *An administrator's guide to preschool inclusion*. Chapel Hill: University of North Carolina, FPG Child Development Center, Early Childhood Research Institute on Inclusion.

Wolery, M., & Wilbers, J. (Eds.). (1994). *Including children with special needs in early childhood programs*. Washington, DC: National Association for the Education of Young Children.

Yelland, N. (Ed.). (2000). *Promoting meaningful learning: Innovations in educating early childhood professionals*. Washington, DC: National Association for the Education of Young Child.

Zimmerman, I. L., Steiner, V. G., & Pond, R. E., (2002). *Preschool Language Scales (PLS-4). English Edition*. San Antonio, TX: Harcourt Assessment.

Appendix A

DEC POSITION STATEMENT ON
DEVELOPMENTAL DELAY

POSITION STATEMENT

ADOPTED: DECEMBER 2005
FIELD REVIEW: OCTOBER 2005

Developmental Delay as an Eligibility Category

DEC believes in the uniqueness of the young child and that services and interventions must be responsive to the young child's needs and patterns of development. We believe that the disability categories used for older school-aged children are often inappropriate for young children birth through eight years and that the category of developmental delay can be a more appropriate designation of disability for special education eligibility. We believe that the assessment of disabilities in young children requires consideration of the whole child through the use of multiple sources, informants, settings and measures.

As defined by DEC in 1991, developmental delay is:

a condition which represents a significant delay in the process of development. It does not refer to a condition in which a child is slightly or momentarily lagging in development. The presence of developmental delay is an indication that the process of development is significantly affected and that without special intervention, it is likely that educational performance at school age will be affected (DEC, 1991, p. 1).

Parent and professional members of DEC believe that a developmental delay category of eligibility should be available from birth through age eight. Though DEC recommends that the category of developmental delay be applied to the period from birth through age eight, we do not disagree with the provision in IDEA 1997 permitting its use for birth through age nine. We believe that the requirement to identify children by traditional disability categories in the early years might result in a premature categorization or miscategorization of children and consequently inappropriate services. Furthermore, the use of the developmental delay category allows for the identification of children with disabilities at younger ages who otherwise might go unserved because of the difficulties in applying traditional disability categories to young children. However, there can be sound reasons for identifying some specific disabilities. This issue is of particular importance for children with multiple or significant disabilities for whom being identified

as developmentally delayed may result in the loss of services, authorization of inappropriate services, or loss of access to adequate or appropriate funding resources. Therefore, the use of a developmental delay category does not preclude the use of appropriate disability categories (e.g., visually impaired, deaf-blind).

Including the developmental delay category as an option from birth through age eight is supported by a number of considerations. First, the period of development typically characterized as early childhood is birth through age eight, a period of development considered to be unique by both the National Association for the Education of Young Children (NAEYC) and DEC. Development in young children is characterized by a broad range of behaviors across developmental domains and is better described by developmental metrics than by those with a more educational or academic focus. Second, using standardized and norm-referenced assessments to identify diagnostic categories for young children continues to result in the incorrect categorization of some children. The psychometric integrity of instruments typically used to classify students for categorical services is only slightly greater for children ages six, seven, and eight than for their younger peers. Third, for many children, the early grades are a crucial foundation for acculturation within the school community. Many children are transient or enter school at kindergarten or beyond. For these children, opportunities to understand and practice school behaviors are limited. Categorical classification during these years would be premature and potentially inaccurate. Fourth, informed team decisions utilizing professional judgments and family input should contribute to eligibility determinations.

Division for Early Childhood
27 Fort Missoula Road • Missoula, MT 59804 • Phone: 406.543.0872 • Fax: 406.543.0887
E-mail: dec@dec-sped.org • www.dec-sped.org

PERMISSION TO COPY NOT REQUIRED – DISTRIBUTION ENCOURAGED

PAGE I OF 2

POSITION STATEMENT: Developmental Delay as an Eligibility Category

Finally, the special education services that children receive have historically been determined by their disability category. Using a developmental delay category for the full span of the early childhood years facilitates a broader, whole-child perspective for intervention. This perspective can focus on the child's needs and the identification of services to meet those needs in developmentally appropriate ways.

DEC is aware of state and local discretion available under IDEA regarding the use of developmental delay as an eligibility category for children ages three through nine. DEC strongly recommends that state and local agencies develop and consistently implement the use of a developmental delay category as an option to insure appropriate services and smooth transitions for children with disabilities and their families during the early childhood period of development. To this end, DEC encourages the use of the category within states and by local school districts. DEC also encourages states to consider the use of a single or aligned state definition of developmental delay for pre-school children served under Section 619 of Part B and for infants and toddlers served under Part C of IDEA.

Division for Early Childhood
27 Fort Missoula Road • Missoula, MT 59804 • Phone: 406.543.0872 • Fax: 406.543.0887
E-mail: dec@dec-sped.org • www.dec-sped.org

PERMISSION TO COPY NOT REQUIRED – DISTRIBUTION ENCOURAGED

Appendix B

DEC AND NAEYC JOINT POSITION
STATEMENT ON INCLUSION

Early Childhood Inclusion

A Joint Position
Statement
of the
Division for
Early Childhood
(DEC) and
the National
Association for
the Education
of Young
Children
(NAEYC)

Today an ever-increasing number of infants and young children with and without disabilities play, develop, and learn together in a variety of places – homes, early childhood programs, neighborhoods, and other community-based settings. The notion that young children with disabilities[1] and their families are full members of the community reflects societal values about promoting opportunities for development and learning, and a sense of belonging for every child. It also reflects a reaction against previous educational practices of separating and isolating children with disabilities. Over time, in combination with certain regulations and protections under the law, these values and societal views regarding children birth to 8 with disabilities and their families have come to be known as early childhood inclusion.[2] The most far-reaching effect of federal legislation on inclusion enacted over the past three decades has been to fundamentally change the way in which early childhood services ideally can be organized and delivered.[3] However, because inclusion takes many different forms and implementation is influenced by a wide variety of factors, questions persist about the precise meaning of inclusion and its implications for policy, practice, and potential outcomes for children and families.

The lack of a shared national definition has contributed to misunderstandings about inclusion. DEC and NAEYC recognize that having a common understanding of what inclusion means is fundamentally important for determining what types of practices and supports are necessary to achieve high quality inclusion. This DEC/NAEYC joint position statement offers a definition of early childhood inclusion. The definition was designed not as a litmus test for determining whether a program can be considered inclusive, but rather, as a blueprint for identifying the key components of high quality inclusive programs. In addition, this document offers recommendations for how the position statement should be used by families, practitioners, administrators, policy makers, and others to improve early childhood services.

Division for Early Childhood of the
Council for Exceptional Children
27 Fort Missoula Road | Missoula, MT 59804
Phone 406.543.0872 | Fax 406.543.0887
Email dec@dec-sped.org | Web www.dec-sped.org

naeyc

National Association for the Education of Young Children
1313 L Street NW, Suite 500 | Washington, DC 20005-4101
Phone 202.232.8777 Toll-Free 800.424.2460 | Fax 202.328.1846
Email naeyc@naeyc.org | Web www.naeyc.org

Definition of Early Childhood Inclusion

Early childhood inclusion embodies the values, policies, and practices that support the right of every infant and young child and his or her family, regardless of ability, to participate in a broad range of activities and contexts as full members of families, communities, and society. The desired results of inclusive experiences for children with and without disabilities and their families include a sense of belonging and membership, positive social relationships and friendships, and development and learning to reach their full potential. The defining features of inclusion that can be used to identify high quality early childhood programs and services are access, participation, and supports.

What is meant by Access, Participation, and Supports?

Access. Providing access to a wide range of learning opportunities, activities, settings, and environments is a defining feature of high quality early childhood inclusion. Inclusion can take many different forms and can occur in various organizational and community contexts, such as homes, Head Start, child care, faith-based programs, recreational programs, preschool, public and private pre-kindergarten through early elementary education, and blended early childhood education/early childhood special education programs. In many cases, simple modifications can facilitate access for individual children. Universal design is a concept that can be used to support access to environments in many different types of settings through the removal of physical and structural barriers. Universal Design for Learning (UDL) reflects practices that provide multiple and varied formats for instruction and learning. UDL principles and practices help to ensure that *every* young child has access to learning environments, to typical home or educational routines and activities, and to the general education curriculum. Technology can enable children with a range of functional abilities to participate in activities and experiences in inclusive settings.

Participation. Even if environments and programs are designed to facilitate access, some children will need additional individualized accommodations and supports to participate fully in play and learning activities with peers and adults. Adults promote belonging, participation, and engagement of children with and without disabilities in inclusive settings in a variety of intentional ways. Tiered models in early childhood hold promise for helping adults organize assessments and interventions by level of intensity. Depending on the individual needs and priorities of young children and families, implementing inclusion involves a range of approaches—from embedded, routines-based teaching to more explicit interventions—to scaffold learning and participation for all children. Social-emotional development and behaviors that facilitate participation are critical goals of high quality early childhood inclusion, along with learning and development in all other domains.

Supports. In addition to provisions addressing access and participation, an infrastructure of systems-level supports must be in place to undergird the efforts of individuals and organizations providing inclusive services to children and families. For example, family members, practitioners, specialists, and administrators should have access to ongoing professional development and support to acquire the knowledge, skills, and dispositions required to implement effective inclusive practices. Because collaboration among key stakeholders (e.g., families, practitioners, specialists, and administrators) is a cornerstone for implementing high quality early childhood inclusion, resources and program policies are needed to promote multiple opportunities for communication and collaboration among these groups. Specialized services and therapies must be implemented in a coordinated fashion and integrated with general early care and education services. Blended early childhood education/early childhood special education programs offer one example of how this might be achieved.[4] Funding policies should promote the

2   Early Childhood Inclusion

APPENDIX B   217 pooling of resources and the use of incentives to increase access to high quality inclusive opportunities. Quality frameworks (e.g., program quality standards, early learning standards and guidelines, and professional competencies and standards) should reflect and guide inclusive practices to ensure that all early childhood practitioners and programs are prepared to address the needs and priorities of infants and young children with disabilities and their families.

Recommendations for Using this Position Statement to Improve Early Childhood Services

Reaching consensus on the meaning of early childhood inclusion is a necessary first step in articulating the field's collective wisdom and values on this critically important issue. In addition, an agreed-upon definition of inclusion should be used to create high expectations for infants and young children with disabilities and to shape educational policies and practices that support high quality inclusion in a wide range of early childhood programs and settings. Recommendations for using this position statement to accomplish these goals include:

1. *Create high expectations for every child to reach his or her full potential.* A definition of early childhood inclusion should help create high expectations for every child, regardless of ability, to reach his or her full potential. Shared expectations can, in turn, lead to the selection of appropriate goals and support the efforts of families, practitioners, individuals, and organizations to advocate for high quality inclusion.

2. *Develop a program philosophy on inclusion.* An agreed-upon definition of inclusion should be used by a wide variety of early childhood programs to develop their own philosophy on inclusion. Programs need a philosophy on inclusion as a part of their broader program mission statement to ensure that

practitioners and staff operate under a similar set of assumptions, values, and beliefs about the most effective ways to support infants and young children with disabilities and their families. A program philosophy on inclusion should be used to shape practices aimed at ensuring that infants and young children with disabilities and their families are full members of the early childhood community and that children have multiple opportunities to learn, develop, and form positive relationships.

3. *Establish a system of services and supports.* Shared understandings about the meaning of inclusion should be the starting point for creating a system of services and supports for children with disabilities and their families. Such a system must reflect a continuum of services and supports that respond to the needs and characteristics of children with varying types of disabilities and levels of severity, including children who are at risk for disabilities. However, the designers of these systems should not lose sight of inclusion as a driving principle and the foundation for the range of services and supports they provide to young children and families. Throughout the service and support system, the goal should be to ensure access, participation, and the infrastructure of supports needed to achieve the desired results related to inclusion. Ideally, the principle of natural proportions should guide the design of inclusive early childhood programs. The principle of natural proportions means the inclusion of children with disabilities in proportion to their presence in the general population. A system of supports and services should include incentives for inclusion, such as child care subsidies, and adjustments to staff-child ratios to ensure that program staff can adequately address the needs of every child.

Early Childhood Inclusion

3

4. ***Revise program and professional standards.*** A definition of inclusion could be used as the basis for revising program and professional standards to incorporate high quality inclusive practices. Because existing early childhood program standards primarily reflect the needs of the general population of young children, improving the overall quality of an early childhood classroom is necessary, but might not be sufficient, to address the individual needs of every child. A shared definition of inclusion could be used as the foundation for identifying dimensions of high quality inclusive programs and the professional standards and competencies of practitioners who work in these settings.

5. ***Achieve an integrated professional development system.*** An agreed-upon definition of inclusion should be used by states to promote an integrated system of high quality professional development to support the inclusion of young children with and without disabilities and their families. The development of such a system would require strategic planning and commitment on the part of families and other key stakeholders across various early childhood sectors (e.g., higher education, child care, Head Start, public pre-kindergarten, preschool, early intervention, health care, mental health). Shared assumptions about the meaning of inclusion are critical for determining who would benefit from professional development, what practitioners need to know and be able to do, and how learning opportunities are organized and facilitated as part of an integrated professional development system.

6. ***Influence federal and state accountability systems.*** Consensus on the meaning of inclusion could influence federal and state accountability standards related to increasing the number of children with disabilities enrolled in inclusive programs. Currently, states are required to report annually to the U.S. Department of Education the number of children with disabilities who are participating in inclusive early childhood programs. But the emphasis on the prevalence of children who receive inclusive services ignores the quality and the anticipated outcomes of the services that children experience. Furthermore, the emphasis on prevalence data raises questions about which types of programs and experiences can be considered inclusive in terms of the intensity of inclusion and the proportion of children with and without disabilities within these settings and activities. A shared definition of inclusion could be used to revise accountability systems to address both the need to increase the number of children with disabilities who receive inclusive services and the goal of improving the quality and outcomes associated with inclusion.

4

Early Childhood Inclusion

Endnotes

1   Phrases such as "children with special needs" and "children with exception-
    alities" are sometimes used in place of "children with disabilities."

2   The term "inclusion" can be used in a broader context relative to opportuni-
    ties and access for children from culturally and linguistically diverse groups,
    a critically important topic in early childhood requiring further discussion
    and inquiry. It is now widely acknowledged, for example, that culture has a
    profound influence on early development and learning, and that early care
    and education practices must reflect this influence. Although this position
    statement is more narrowly focused on inclusion as it relates to disability, it
    is understood that children with disabilities and their families vary widely with
    respect to their racial/ethnic, cultural, economic, and linguistic backgrounds.

3   In accordance with the Individuals with Disabilities Education Act (IDEA),
    children ages 3-21 are entitled to a free, appropriate public education (FAPE)
    in the least restrictive environment (LRE). LRE requires that, to the extent
    possible, children with disabilities should have access to the general educa-
    tion curriculum, along with learning activities and settings that are available
    to their peers without disabilities. Corresponding federal legislation ap-
    plied to infants and toddlers (children birth to 3) and their families specifies
    that early intervention services and supports must be provided in "natural
    environments," generally interpreted to mean a broad range of contexts and
    activities that generally occur for typically developing infants and toddlers in
    homes and communities. Although this document focuses on the broader
    meaning and implications of early childhood inclusion for children birth to
    eight, it is recognized that the basic ideas and values reflected in the term
    "inclusion" are congruent with those reflected in the term "natural environ-
    ments." Furthermore, it is acknowledged that fundamental concepts related
    to both inclusion and natural environments extend well beyond the early
    childhood period to include older elementary school students and beyond.

4   Blended programs integrate key components (e.g., funding, eligibility criteria,
    curricula) of two or more different types of early childhood programs (e.g.,
    the federally funded program for preschoolers with disabilities [Part B-619] in
    combination with Head Start, public pre-k, and/or child care) with the goal of
    serving a broader group of children and families within a single program.

Early Childhood Inclusion   5

APPROVED BY DEC EXECUTIVE BOARD: April 2009

APPROVED BY NAEYC GOVERNING BOARD: April 2009

Suggested citation
DEC/NAEYC. (2009). *Early childhood inclusion: A joint position statement of the Division for Early Childhood (DEC) and the National Association for the Education of Young Children (NAEYC).* Chapel Hill: The University of North Carolina, FPG Child Development Institute.

Permission to copy not required — distribution encouraged.

http://community.fpg.unc.edu/resources/articles/Early_Childhood_Inclusion

Acknowledgments
Coordination of the development and validation of this joint position statement was provided by the National Professional Development Center on Inclusion (NPDCI), a project of the FPG Child Development Institute funded by a grant from the U.S. Department of Education, Office of Special Education Programs. NPDCI work group members included Camille Catlett, who directed the validation process, Virginia Buysse, who served as the lead writer, and Heidi Hollingsworth, who supervised the analysis of respondent comments and the editorial process.

DEC and NAEYC appreciate the work of Joint DEC-NAEYC Work Group members who participated in the development of the initial definition and position statement: Terry Harrison, NJ Department of Health and Senior Services; Helen Keith, University of Vermont; Louise Kaczmarek, University of Pittsburgh; Robin McWilliam, Siskin Children's Institute and the University of Tennessee at Chattanooga; Judy Niemeyer, University of North Carolina at Greensboro; Cheryl Rhodes, Georgia State University; Bea Vargas, El Papalote Inclusive Child Development Center; and Mary Wonderlick, consultant. Input from the members of the DEC Executive Board and the NAEYC Governing Board, as well as key staff members in both organizations, also is acknowledged.

6   Early Childhood Inclusion

Appendix C

ANNOTATED WEB RESOURCES

American Association on Intellectual and Developmental Disabilities

http://www.aamr.org

The American Association on Intellectual and Developmental Disabilities (AAIDD) defines the disability and provides resources for classroom teachers and other professionals working with children who need assistance. The organization, formerly known as the American Association of Mental Retardation, also develops public policy initiatives in support of individuals with developmental disabilities. The site offers position papers ranging from aging, to employment, to sexuality in individuals who possess the disability.

American Society for Deaf Children

http://www.deafchildren.org

The American Society for Deaf Children (ASDC) provides information for parents and professionals about deafness. Resources are available, and links are shared for other deafness and hard of hearing Web sites.

American Speech-Language-Hearing Association

http://www.asha.org

The American Speech-Language-Hearing Association (ASHA) is an international professional organization for speech, language, and hearing specialists. It offers continuing education courses that meet state licensing requirements.

Council for Exceptional Children

http://www.cec.sped.org

The Council for Exceptional Children Web site lists several topics related to teachers' understanding of children with special needs. Check out the links for "Current Special Ed Topics" and "Evidence-based Practice" for information that affects classrooms, curriculum, and daily planning.

Children and Adults with Attention Deficit/Hyperactivity Disorder

http://www.chadd.org

Children and Adults with Attention Deficit/Hyperactivity Disorder (CHADD), founded in 1987, represents individuals with ADHD. ADHD is a potentially serious medical disorder, affecting up to 3% to 5% of all children. Children with ADHD are eligible for special education services or accommodations in regular classrooms. CHADD is a nonprofit national organization for children and adults with ADHD.

Circle of Inclusion

http://www.circleofinclusion.org

This site shares information about effective practices of inclusive educational programs for children from birth through age 8.

The Division for Early Childhood

http://www.dec-sped.org

The Division for Early Childhood (DEC), a division of the Council for Exceptional Children, focuses on children with special needs from birth through age 8 and their families. You can find position statements and a Recommended Practices section on this site.

Disability Is Natural

http://www.disabilityisnatural.com

Visit this site to develop new ways of thinking about children with disabilities.

Federation for Children with Special Needs

http://www.fcsn.org

The Federation for Children with Special Needs provides a Family Resource Database for parents. Its overall mission is "Informing, Educating, Empowering Families." The site includes links to other helpful sites, such as the National Dissemination Center for Children with Disabilities.

Frank Porter Graham Center

http://www.fpg.unc.edu

The Frank Porter Graham Center (FPG) at the University of North Carolina is devoted to the study of children and families, focusing on children who possess biological or environmental factors that challenge early development and learning. The center disseminates knowledge to both families and professionals.

HearingCenterOnline.com

http://www.hearingcenteronline.com

This site provides information about hearing products and technology support for the hearing impaired.

Kids Together, Inc.

http://www.kidstogether.org

Kids Together, Inc., a nonprofit organization founded by parents, seeks "to promote inclusion communities where all people belong." The site defines inclusion, includes the full text of the Individuals with Disabilities Education Act, and provides other helpful resources for children and adults.

MAAP Services for Autism and Asperger Syndrome

http://www.maapservices.org

MAAP Services for Autism and Asperger Syndrome, a nonprofit organization, provides information to families of individuals with autism, Asperger's syndrome, and pervasive developmental disorder (PDD). The site defines legal rights for individuals who have autism and related conditions and shares information about subscriptions to "The MAAP" quarterly newsletter.

National Association for the Education of Young Children

http://www.naeyc.org

The National Association for the Education of Young Children (NAEYC) is committed to the education of young children birth through age 8 and to defining high-quality care for this population. Publications are available including an online position statement on inclusion, a research monograph, and other publications that address issues concerning planning and implementing appropriate programs for children with disabilities.

National Center to Improve Practice in Special Education Through Technology, Media and Materials

http://www2.edc.org/NCIP

The National Center to Improve Practice in Special Education Through Technology, Media and Materials (NCIP) shares information about technological resources for children with special needs. Video clips are available showing children using assistive and instructional technology, and two "guided tours" show exemplary early childhood classrooms in action. Teachers would benefit by accessing this site.

The National Child Care Information and Technical Assistance Center

http://www.nccic.org/index.html

The National Child Care Information and Technical Assistance Center (NCCIC), a branch of the U.S. Department of Health and Human Services, links parents, providers, and the public to early care and education information. Important links to clearinghouses and national organizations are available on the site.

National Council on Disability

http://www.ncd.gov

The National Council on Disability is an independent federal agency that assists families in knowing their rights. Under the Resources section on the site is helpful information about contacting U.S. senators and representatives to lobby for legislation regarding children with special needs.

National Early Childhood Technical Assistance Center

http://www.nectac.org

Choose the "Topic Pages" link on this site to read information related to implementing the early childhood provisions for IDEA (2004). This site also includes information about national organizations and resources related to inclusion.

National Federation of the Blind

http://www.nfb.org

The National Federation of the Blind (NFB) is the largest organization in the United States representing people who are blind. NFB has more than 700 local affiliates in all 50 states plus Washington, DC, and Puerto Rico. The group seeks to improve the lives of blind people through advocacy, education, research, and technology.

National Dissemination Center for Children with Disabilities

http://www.nichcy.org

The National Dissemination Center for Children with Disabilities is a rich source of information about effective educational practices for infants, toddlers, children and youth, IDEA, and No Child Left Behind. Documents are available in English and Spanish.

Orelena Hawks Puckett Institute

http://www.puckett.org

The Orelena Hawks Puckett Institute, a not-for-profit organization, conducts research activities to encourage and strengthen child, parent, and family development in positive ways.

Partners in Policymaking

http://www.partnersinpolicymaking.com

Partners in Policymaking, a site developed in by the Minnesota Governor's Council on Developmental Disabilities, offers online courses designed to educate families about developmental disabilities and working with children who have special needs. The courses, protected by privacy rights, are self-directed and free of charge.

PEAK Parent Center

http://www.peakparent.org

The PEAK Parent Center provides training, information, and technical assistance to support families of children from birth through age 26. They advocate for training on inclusive education and offer resources for educating all children in general education classrooms.

Power of the Ordinary

http://www.poweroftheordinary.org

Power of the Ordinary is a project sponsored by the Center for Dissemination and Utilization of the Orelena Hawks Puckett Institute that shares a variety of information about children with disabilities.

Preschool Options Project

http://www.preschooloptions.org/resources/index.php

The Wisconsin Department of Public Instruction shares a reference list of articles, books, pamphlets, brochures, and other resources as part of its Preschool Options Project. The site is appropriate for parents and teachers alike.

Technical Assistance Alliance for Parent Centers

http://www.taalliance.org

The U.S. Department of Education, Office of Special Education Programs provides one national and six regional Technical Assistance Alliance for Parent Centers under the Individuals with Disabilities Education Act (IDEA). This innovative project supports a system that develops and coordinates parent training and information projects. The purpose of the centers is to unify and strengthen partnerships between parent centers and state education systems.

Therapists as Collaborative Team members for Infant/Toddler Community Services

http://tactics.fsu.edu

Therapists as Collaborative Team members for Infant/Toddler Community Services (TaCTICS) is an outreach training project funded by the U.S. Department of Education that provides useful information for service providers about Part C Services. Professionals who use the site are able to assess the child's/family's daily routines to plan intervention activities.

TASH

http://www.tash.org/index.html

TASH (formerly The Association for Persons with Severe Handicaps) is an international association that advocates for people with disabilities. Its membership, composed of people with disabilities, family members, professionals, and advocates, works together so that all people are included in all aspects of society.

The Arc

http://www.thearc.org

The Arc provides information to the childcare industry about the Americans with Disabilities Act (ADA), including accommodations that facilitate working with children who have a wide range of disabilities. Information is available in both Spanish and English.

Zero to Three

http://www.zerotothree.org/site/PageServer

Zero to Three, a national nonprofit organization, is a national center for infants, toddlers, and families. The mission of the group is to promote healthy development of young children by supporting and strengthening families and those who work with them. Many publications and reports are available through the center to provide information about best practices in homes and childcare centers.